LEARNING STYLES INVENTORY

—

VERSION III

A MEASURE OF STUDENT PREFERENCES FOR INSTRUCTIONAL TECHNIQUES

TECHNICAL AND ADMINISTRATION MANUAL

JOSEPH S. RENZULLI
MARY G. RIZZA
LINDA H. SMITH

Editor
Rachel A. Knox

Creative Learning Press, Inc.
P.O. Box 320, Mansfield Center, CT 06250
888-518-8004 • www.creativelearningpress.com

Table of Contents

List of Tables

Introduction and Overview

The *Learning Styles Inventory, Version III* (*LSI-III*) is an instrument that is designed to measure student preferences for instructional strategies commonly found in elementary and middle school classrooms. This new version of the *LSI* includes two instruments, one designed for elementary school students (*LSI-III/ES*) and one for middle school students (*LSI-III/MS*). The *LSI-III/ES* contains 56 questions and the *LSI-III/MS* contains 62 questions. Each instrument takes approximately 15 minutes to complete. (This version of the *LSI* also includes a teacher instrument based on the student instruments. However, it was not subjected to the same validity and reliability studies as the student instruments.) The *Learning Styles Inventory, Version III* has been successfully used to help create a more responsive learning environment for individuals and small groups of students in grades three through eight. The instruments presented in this manual are the third revision of an instrument originally published in 1978 (Renzulli and Smith, 1978).

Part I of this manual is reproducible, and each teacher who administers the *LSI-III* should receive a copy. Part I addresses the following four questions:

- What is the *LSI-III* and what does it measure?
- How do I administer and score the *LSI-III*?
- How do I interpret my students' scores on the *LSI-III?*
- How can I alter my teaching styles to accommodate my students' learning styles?

We have included key resources for teachers who would like to further explore ways in which their teaching can be more responsive to individual differences that exist among their students. In addition, teachers should have access to and be encouraged to study the appendices included in this manual.

Part II of this manual consists of the research that we carried out to establish the technical qualities of this revised edition of the *LSI* and includes sections that describe the content validity, the construct validity, and the reliability.

Because we wanted to develop a manual and instrument that is easy for teachers and administrators to use and understand, we did not crowd the practical sections of the manual with large amounts of research and theoretical information. However, we consider this information to be very important, especially for individuals who want to prepare a rationale for using the *LSI-III* or for those who have an advanced interest in theory and research. We have included this information in the appendices.

Appendix A describes the theoretical rationale and underlying research that supports the usefulness of information about student learning styles. We review major theoretical perspectives on human abilities, interests, and styles—all critical concepts for understanding the diversity in individuals' approaches to learning tasks. We believe that these concepts are interrelated in many ways and best understood in the contexts in which they are observed and measured. In other words, a student's abilities, interests, and styles are not static, and teachers can make modifications to the curriculum and the range of instructional styles they employ in the classroom in order to capitalize on developed and developing abilities, interests and styles. The *Learning Styles Inventory, Version III* represents a practical application of this perspective as it helps teachers recognize the particular learning styles that their students prefer.

Because the *LSI-III* addresses only one part of how a student engages in an act of learning, Appendix B describes other instruments that can help educators develop and examine a more complete picture of student abilities, interests, and learning and expression styles—including the *Interest-A-Lyzer* family of instruments (Renzulli, 1977, 1997; Renzulli & Rizza, 1997), *Scales for Rating Behavioral Characteristics of Superior Students* (Renzulli et al., 2002), and *My Way: An Expression Styles Inventory* (Kettle, Renzulli, & Rizza, 1998)—and explains how teachers can put all this and other student information together in a Total Talent Portfolio (Purcell & Renzulli, 1998). (Appendix C presents sample pages from these instruments.) By analyzing the total student picture compiled in the Total Talent Portfolio, educators can then make informed curricular and instructional modifications that capitalize on students strengths, needs, and interests.

Finally, Appendix D includes samples of both the elementary and middle school instruments of the *LSI-III* as well as the teacher edition. To obtain classroom sets of the instruments, contact Creative Learning Press, Inc. (888-518-8004; www.creativelearningpress.com).

While the purpose of the *LSI-III* is to identify students' learning style preferences, educators should make every effort to avoid stamping a child with a learning style in the manner that some children are labeled according to intelligence level or disability. In rare cases certain students may prefer to pursue most of their studies through a single method such as independent study, but the majority of learners vary their preferences for different instructional techniques based on their age and the subject matter. We therefore recommend that the *LSI-III* be readministered at various intervals in a student's academic career so that teachers can document and accommodate changes in individual preferences.

PART I

USING THE *LEARNING STYLES INVENTORY, VERSION III* IN THE CLASSROOM

The *Learning Styles Inventory, Version III* (*LSI-III*) is a valuable tool for identifying student preferences for particular instructional techniques. This brief introduction explains how to administer, score, and use the *Learning Styles Inventory* and addresses the following questions:

- What is the *LSI-III* and what does it measure?
- How do I administer and score the *LSI-III*?
- How do I interpret my students' scores on the *LSI-III?*
- How can I alter my teaching styles to accommodate my students' learning styles?

What is the *LSI-III* and what does it measure?

The **Learning Styles Inventory** is designed to measure student preferences for nine instructional strategies commonly found in elementary and middle school classrooms. This new version of the *LSI* includes two instruments, one designed for elementary school students (*LSI-III/ES*) and one for middle school students (*LSI-III/MS*). The *LSI-III/ES* contains 56 questions and the *LSI-III/MS* contains 62 questions. Each instrument takes approximately 15 minutes to complete. The *Learning Styles Inventory, Version III* has been successfully used to plan instruction for students in grades three through eight.

The nine learning styles defined by the *LSI-III* include:

Direct Instruction

Direct instruction refers to a verbal presentation in which the teacher or an expert in a particular field communicates ideas and concepts. The direct instruction method includes having the teacher present a lesson, explain new information, and present various viewpoints. The factor also contains items that include having the teacher give directions and lead discussions.

Instruction through Technology

The items on this factor are all related to the use of computers and other educational technology. Using computers to learn new information, review information, and participate in interactive activities are included on this factor. Activities that involve the Internet as well as communicating via e-mail and in chat rooms are also the subject of some items. In addition, video and television broadcasts are included in this factor.

Simulations

This approach attempts to teach content and skills through role playing. Simulations invite students to assume roles and explore real-world situations. Students who obtain a high score on this style prefer to learn material within concrete/real-life experiences.

Projects

The project method invites students to work on school-related, group activities that are either student initiated or teacher directed. Students who obtain a high score on this style prefer to work in groups and on projects independent from the curriculum.

Independent Study

In an independent study, individual students pursue a topic or area of study on their own. Typically, students choose an area of study, develop their own approach to gathering information, and compile the results in a presentation or product. Students who obtain a high score on this style prefer to work alone.

Peer Teaching

In peer teaching, students teach other students a particular topic or skill. Students who obtain a high score on this style are comfortable seeking help from peers and enjoy working with other students when practicing or studying.

Drill & Recitation (elementary school instrument only)

This traditional approach to instruction involves a teacher asking questions and calling on students to respond with appropriate information. Students who obtain a high score on this style prefer to demonstrate their knowledge of content areas by verbal recitation.

Discussion (middle school instrument only)

Discussion is characterized by a two-way interaction between teacher and students or among students. Students who obtain a high score on this style prefer to listen to or participate in exchanges of information and opinions verbally.

Teaching Games (middle school instrument only)

This technique invites students to acquire and transfer knowledge within the context of a game. Students who obtain a high score on this style prefer to compete in activities in which they receive immediate feedback on their performance.

How do I administer and score the *LSI-III*?

Administering and scoring the *Learning Styles Inventory, Version III* has never been easier. We have taken information and suggestions from field tests of the instrument and redesigned the forms to help make the *LSI-III* an easy-to-use and informative tool. In addition to this new format, the *LSI-III* is now self-scoring. You and your students can quickly score and analyze results, allowing you to apply the results to your instruction immediately.

We suggest that you read over each item on the instrument in order to anticipate any questions your students may have about the interpretation of individual items. We have included the definitions of each learning style to help you interpret the intent of an item and help you answer any questions your students may have.

When administering the *LSI-III,* first read aloud the directions on the front of the instrument. Be sure students understand that their preferred choice is based on whether the item describes an activity that interests them, not if they have had experience with the activity. Whether or not you incorporate similar activities in your classroom should not influence the preferred choice of your students. This instrument is a learning experience for students and teachers alike. It is just as important for the students as it is for you, the teacher, to understand their learning preferences.

Review the definitions of the scoring options. Although the differences may seem obvious, take a moment to check that your students understand the difference between each response category (Really Like, Like, Not Sure, Dislike, Really Dislike). In addition, you should emphasize to your students that they read each item and indicate their preferences based on that item alone, not in conjunction with other items. This instrument is not a ranking of items, but a discrete decision of student preference for one particular item.

After students have circled their responses for each item, they should add up the circled numbers in each section. Students should turn to the "Section Totals" table on the last page of the instrument and circle the score or range of scores that matches or includes their total score for each section. We suggest that you circulate among students during the scoring process since each student will complete the form at her or his own pace and may have individual questions regarding proper procedure.

We have also included a classroom summary sheet designed to help you chart or organize students' scores. This sheet allows you to transfer style scores to a grid that displays the whole class at a glance. This summary sheet will be helpful in providing a quick reference guide to all student scores.

How do I interpret my students' scores on the *LSI-III*?

The most important thing to keep in mind when scoring the *LSI-III* is that this instrument is *not* a test and there are no norms against which you can make comparisons between and among various groups. The main purpose of the instrument is to gain information about students as individuals and to use this information to make programming rather than classification decisions. Rough estimates about what the scores mean were determined from our research studies. Using information from the research sample population that participated in the reliability and validity studies underlying the instrument, we were able to calculate means and standard deviations for each dimension of the *LSI-III*. The raw data were then converted to t-scores for each subscale. T-scores (which have a Mean of 50 and a Standard Deviation of 10) allow responses to be compared across factors that contain different numbers of items. Each t-score, therefore, corresponds to a total subscale score or range of scores depending on the factor. In order to facilitate interpretation, the t-scores were then transformed into converted scores of 1-10. The converted scores have a Mean = 5 and SD = 2. These scores allow teachers, students, and parents to use the following ranges as a very general guide for interpreting the scores.

Converted Score	Preference Level
9-10	Very High
7-8	High
5-6	Average
3-4	Low
1-2	Very Low

In addition to looking at your students' general style scores, we suggest that you read through each student's *LSI-III* to get a better understanding of his or her pattern of answers as well as specific preferences. This process is particularly important for students who appear to exhibit no interest in any factor. The *LSI-III* asks for preferences on some very specific activities, and some students may prefer specific types of activities that are only one aspect of an entire style. For example, a student may prefer to work in groups and on panels within a real-life situation such as a simulation, but many of the items in this style discuss acting out roles—activities that may not be a preference for that student. He or she may still enjoy simulations, but only within a group setting.

You may want to use the results of an *LSI-III* as the subject of teacher/student conferences and have students tell you what they think of the instrument. Once they see the style structure, they may have opinions of their style preferences that they did not initially recognize.

How can I alter my teaching styles to accommodate my students' learning styles?

The items on the *LSI-III* describe general activities found within the nine categories of learning styles and focus on the instructional practices commonly used in elementary and middle school classrooms. In order to make the most of the information gained from administering the *LSI-III*, you should strive to match your instructional practices to students' preferred learning styles whenever appropriate. A teacher edition of the *LSI-III* allows you to compare your strategy use directly to your students' preferences. It is based on the items found on each of the student versions and asks you to rate how often you employ the activities and strategies found on the student instruments. The scoring is slightly different on the teacher version: After rating each item, you will calculate an average for each factor by adding your scores into a raw score and dividing by the number of items. To obtain your mean score for each factor, round up after averaging. Interpreting your scores is easily accomplished by comparing your mean scores on each factor to the following chart:

Frequency	Score	Rating
Daily	4	Very High
Weekly	3	High
Monthly	2	Moderate
Occasionally	1	Low
Never	0	Very Low

There are a number of ways in which you can employ a wider variety of teaching strategies to accommodate student preferences. For example, during some lessons, you may want to group students according to style and allow each group to complete activities that take advantage of the group's preferred learning style. Mrs. Shobe, a 4th grade enrichment teacher used the information obtained from the *LSI-III* to differentiate a unit on parts of speech. She worked at the overhead projector with a small group on an activity that used movie reviews with the adjectives removed (Direct Instruction). At the same time, a few students worked at the computer stations on a story-writing program called Wacky Web Tales (http://www.eduplace.com/tales/) that reinforced their use of different parts of speech (Instruction through Technology and Independent Study). Three students worked together designing a scavenger hunt for their classmates using abstract and concrete nouns (Projects and Peer Teaching). Later, the whole class participated in a kinesthetic activity that required them to listen to a short story and perform specific actions when they heard a different part of speech (e.g., hearing a noun prompted a raised right hand, a verb required touching the nose, and an adjective indicated a left hand on the head). Students were eliminated "Simon Says" style (Drill & Recitation and Teaching Games). While Mrs. Shobe was not able to accommodate all styles, she allowed the students to choose an activity that closely approximated the preferences indicated by their *LSI-III*. In short, even though you can't please all students all of the time, the *LSI-III* provides valuable information that allows you to implement some variety within a classroom that will accommodate most students most of the time.

How you use the information obtained on the *LSI-III* depends upon your comfort level with change in your classroom. Some teachers have used information gathered from the *LSI-III* to radically alter their mode of teaching. In response to her students' preferences, one teacher changed the organizational structure of her classroom to allow students a choice to work either in small groups or independently, rather than as a whole class. We suggest that you incorporate new strategies in accordance with your own teaching style. The more comfortable you are with a new strategy, the smoother the transition will be for the students. Start small and measure your success one day at a time. Above all, don't get discouraged. Change is a process that takes time.

Whether you are incorporating new strategies into your curriculum or altering how you use established strategies, the outcome is the same—a more inviting and exciting classroom for you and your students. In the section that follows, we have listed a number of instructional strategies that teachers have found useful in accommodating various learning styles[1]. In addition, we have provided a list of key references for enhancing instruction techniques in a learning styles oriented classroom. The most important thing to remember is that the individual style(s) of a student should always be viewed as a *strength* that can make learning more engaging, efficient, and enjoyable.

Direct Instruction

❖ Provide graphic organizers by having students identify key information that is then categorized in meaningful ways. Information can be classified under a heading and related to the nucleus word or words that identify a primary topic. Vary the graphic organizers to reflect the sequence of events, causal relations, and interactions between problems and their solutions.

❖ Teach effective note-taking skills by dividing the notepaper in half. On one side of the paper generate questions and on the other half provide the information to answer the questions.

❖ Provide handouts of information covered.

❖ Alternate between lecture and questions.

❖ Have students summarize information or react to information after short periods of lecturing.

❖ Describe the topic in terms of its parallels to experiences and examples with which the students are likely to be familiar.

❖ Provide examples and nonexamples of the concepts being introduced (concept attainment strategy).

❖ Ask students to provide examples and nonexamples of the concepts being introduced (concept attainment strategy).

❖ Infuse storytelling into the lecture format.

❖ Invite guest speakers to address the class and share what they know about a topic.

❖ Use a variety of print and media resources to elaborate on or underscore a particular point.

❖ Include a demonstration or a presentation with slides.

❖ Assist students in forming concepts by asking open-ended questions designed to elicit as much data as possible. Ask students to record the class' answers, organize the information into groups, and assign conceptual labels. For example, prior to a unit on democracy, you might ask, "What do you think of when you hear the word democracy?" Students generate responses, organize the information into groups, and assign conceptual labels to explain the attributes of the groups (concept formation/diagnosis).

❖ Have students use manipulatives to facilitate an understanding of a concept.

Instruction through Technology

❖ Create a Webquest or website and structure it so that students can work through a concept at their own pace.

❖ Use software tutorials as a form of programmed instruction.

❖ Establish clear rules for Internet use and have students sign contracts that make them responsible for their own behavior.

---

[1] Information adapted from Renzulli, J. S., Leppien, J. H., & Hays, T. S. (2000). *The Multiple Menu Model: A Practical Guide for Developing Differentiated Curriculum.*

- ❖ Allow students time to search sites of their own interest while finding information for your assignment. Remember that your assignments are thought provoking and may spark tangential interest in students that they can easily follow using the Internet. Try not to stop their curiosity, but keep them accountable for the work at hand.

- ❖ Remember that technology is a means to an end and should enhance the project at hand. Evaluate the use of technology by asking if the task could be accomplished as well without the technology.

Simulations

- ❖ Require students to assume roles, make decisions, and face the consequences of their actions.

- ❖ Provide time to introduce students to the simulation and time to explore their assigned roles and plot strategies.

- ❖ Play an active role in facilitating the process and debriefing the simulation through discussion.

- ❖ Design a problem or situation that is useful for exploring a particular concept. Design background information or have students investigate the background information that will assist them in carrying out their roles.

- ❖ Engage students in debates that engage them in exploring opposing viewpoints.

- ❖ Have students play a role on a panel or forum to explore an idea or concept.

- ❖ Provide opportunities for students to dramatize an event, situation, or system. For example, in science class, students can investigate the function of various parts of a plant, organ, or solar system by role-playing the functions.

Projects

- ❖ Assist students in identifying problems and formulating research plans.

- ❖ Help students identify what they know and don't know about a problem or project topic.

- ❖ Provide students with resources, both traditional and nontraditional, that may assist them with their projects. For example, help them identify experts in related fields that they can interview to obtain background information.

- ❖ Provide methodological support to assist student in gathering and analyzing information. For example, teach students how to conduct interviews, design surveys, detect bias in sources, etc.

Independent Study

- ❖ Assist student in pursuing real problems that have the following characteristics:

  - ❖ Students have an emotional or internal commitment in addition to a cognitive or scholarly interest in pursuing the problem.

  - ❖ The real problem does not have existing or unique solutions. This characteristic differentiates the problem from an exercise.

  - ❖ Students want to bring about some form of change in actions, attitudes, or beliefs in a targeted audience, or they want to contribute something new to the sciences, arts, or humanities.

  - ❖ The product or service is directed toward a specific, authentic audience (e.g., local historical society).

- ❖ Introduce students to various methodological and domain-specific skills to explore topics as practicing professionals would study them.

- ❖ Arrange for students to meet with individuals/mentors who might assist them in acquiring information.

Peer Teaching
- ❖ Pair students who share similar interests or in situations in which each person mutually benefits from the information shared.

- ❖ Have students become experts in particular topics so that they can share this information with other students who have selected other topics to pursue.

- ❖ Try to establish opportunities for all students to show their expertise.

Drill & Recitation
- ❖ Teach specific strategies for recalling information (e.g., identifying principles that are shared by information being memorized, looking for relationships between the elements being learned, placing information within a contextual setting).

- ❖ Encourage students to categorize information based on attributes.

- ❖ Include game formats to strengthen student interest.

- ❖ Teach students to run their own practice sessions. Help them learn strategies for practicing their spelling words and then let students practice with each other.

Discussion
- ❖ Vary the level of questions that you ask.

- ❖ Provide wait-time before allowing a student to give a response and after hearing a response from the group.

- ❖ Listen to what students are trying to explain and follow up their responses with clarifying questions.

- ❖ Vary the strategies to engage students in discussion. Provide students with a set of questions that the class will explore and give them time to prepare their responses individually or in small groups.

- ❖ Allow students to generate their own questions about a topic or concept and encourage them to ask questions of each other. For example, let the students organize their own discussion groups and require them to ask questions of each other.

- ❖ Place students in literary discussion groups and allow them to generate a series of questions to ask each other about the book that they have read. Teach students to generate interpretive and evaluative questions.

Teaching Games
- ❖ Provide a variety of options from which students can choose.

- ❖ Avoid having the games be a reward for behavior. They should be available for all students because they reinforce the skills and content you are highlighting in your curriculum.

- ❖ Allow students to design their own games with the requirement that they use or test accurate and relevant knowledge.

Key References

- ❖ Bluestein, J. (Ed.). (1995). *Mentors, masters and Mrs. MacGregor: Stories of teachers making a difference*. Deerfield Beach, FL: Health Communications.

  A common characteristic between great teachers mentioned in this compilation is that they all made the effort to reach out to individual students. These reflections from students underscore that the process of learning matters as much as (if not more than) the content.

- ❖ Burns, D. E. (1990). *Pathways to investigative skills: Instructional lessons for guiding students from problem finding to final product* . Storrs, CT: Creative Learning Press, Inc.

  One way to actively engage students in their own education is to allow them opportunities to pursue authentic projects of their own choosing. *Pathways* presents 10 lessons that guide teachers and students through the process of finding real-world areas of research, developing the skills to pursue the research, and creating and presenting a final product.

- ❖ Gardner, H. (2000). *Intelligence reframed: Multiple intelligences for the 21st century*. New York: Basic Books.

  The more teachers know about their students, the better they will be able to address their needs in the classroom. Gardner's Multiple Intelligences theory offers a framework for understanding a wider range of abilities and talents than can be tested on IQ tests.

- ❖ Purcell, J. H., & Renzulli, J. S. (1998). *Total talent portfolio: A systematic plan to identify and nurture gifts and talents*. Storrs, CT: Creative Learning Press, Inc.

  By gathering information about students' abilities, interests, and styles, educators can work to develop appropriate learning experiences that challenge and engage each student. *Total Talent Portfolio* outlines what kinds of information teachers and students should gather into a portfolio and how to turn the information into plans and goals that nurture each student's interests and talents.

- ❖ Reis, S. M., Burns, D. E., & Renzulli, J. S. (1992). *Curriculum compacting: The complete guide to modifying the regular curriculum for high ability students*. Storrs, CT: Creative Learning Press, Inc.

  Bright students often master the regular curriculum more quickly than others. By compacting the curriculum for those students into fewer lessons, educators can then offer enrichment activities to students that allow them to explore topics in more depth.

- ❖ Renzulli, J. S., Leppien, J. H., & Hays, T. S. (2000). *The multiple menu model: A practical guide for developing differentiated curriculum*. Storrs, CT: Creative Learning Press, Inc.

  Teachers can make learning more meaningful, relevant, and exciting by presenting topics within real-world contexts and engaging their students as authentic researchers. Six "menus" guide educators through developing student activities, employing a range of teaching strategies, injecting creative contributions into the curriculum, and offering students options in how they present their understanding.

- ❖ Renzulli, J. S., & Reis, S. M. (1997). *The schoolwide enrichment model: A how-to guide for educational excellence* (2nd ed.). Storrs, CT: Creative Learning Press, Inc.

  The Schoolwide Enrichment Model shows schools how to treat students as individuals and nurture interests and abilities (developed and developing) without creating chaos in the classroom. This practical resource provides teacher training activities, action forms, advice for modifying the curriculum and much more.

- ❖ Tomlinson, C. A. (1999). *The differentiated classroom: Responding to the needs of all learners*. Alexandria, VA: Association for Supervision and Curriculum Development.

  The Differentiated Classroom presents the theory underlying differentiation as well as practical advice for providing differentiated instruction in the regular classroom. Three chapters illustrate differentiation in action through examples of actual lessons, units, and classrooms.

❖ Tomlinson, C. A. (2001). *How to differentiate instruction in mixed-ability classrooms* (2nd ed.). Alexandria, VA: Association for Supervision and Curriculum Development.

Because not all students learn at the same pace and in the same way, Tomlinson shows teachers how to match instructional approaches to student readiness, interests, and talents by differentiating instruction. Strategies include curriculum compacting, "sidebar" investigations, contracts, graphic organizers, and portfolios.

PART II

DEVELOPMENT OF THE *LEARNING STYLES INVENTORY, VERSION III*

Instrumentation

Content Validity

The questions contained in the final version of the *Learning Styles Inventory, Version III* are the result of a lengthy process that began with a review of the items found on the original instrument. We obtained feedback from users of the instrument (e.g., classroom teachers) who reported that some of the items did not match what they did in their classrooms. For example, the items contained in the Programmed Instruction factor were often questioned by students who did not have these experiences. We also received suggestions to add items that reflected the influence of technology in the classroom.

Experts in the field of gifted education analyzed the items. A group of university professors, graduate students, and classroom teachers reviewed original and new items to determine appropriateness for elementary and middle school classrooms in addition to how well each item fit with the proposed factor structure. Items on the new instrument were designed as follows:

First, we changed the gerund phrases used throughout the instrument to infinitive phrases. For example, we rewrote "Sharing ideas with other students during a class discussion of some topic" to "Share ideas with other students during a class discussion." In item 5, we modified "Being a member of a panel that is discussing current events" to "Take part in a panel to discuss current events." We also shortened some items to eliminate confusion. For example, "Having other students who are experts on a topic present their ideas to the class" became "Have other students present their ideas to the class." Other examples are listed below.

- "Having a friend help you learn material you are finding difficult to understand" *became* "Have a friend help you learn difficult material."

- "Having the teacher ask the class questions on work that was assigned to be studied" *became* "Have the teacher ask the class questions on assigned work."

- "Practicing vocabulary words by playing a game such as Password" *became* "Practice vocabulary words by playing a word game."

- "Working on assignments where you fill in the missing word to complete a sentence" *became* "Fill in the missing word to complete a sentence on an assignment."

- "Learning about the election process by playing the role of a member of a campaign team competing with another team to win votes for your candidate" *became*

"Learn about the election process by playing the role of a member of a campaign team."

- "Learning new information or learning how to solve a problem from another student in your class" *became*
  "Learn new information from another student in your class."

- "Learning how government works by playing the role of an official who must deal with a crisis situation" *became*
  "Learn how government works by playing the role of an official working with a local citizen group."

- "Having the teacher call on individual students to recite such things as multiplication tables or the names of past presidents of the United States" *became*
  "Have your teacher call on individual students to recite information that you have learned."

- "Having a spelling bee where your team is trying to out-spell another team" *became*
  "Have a spelling bee with other students in your class."

We also dropped or changed other items. We eliminated "Discussing an issue because you disagree with what another student has said" because of the negative connotation. We thought the item "Working on assignments that have many questions but ones that you are likely to get right" was similar to another question and dropped it. Finally, we drastically altered one item to reflect the influx of technology: "Doing research in the library for a paper you want to write" became "Search sources in the library or on the Internet for information about a topic you are studying."

We developed twenty-two additional items to test the influence of grouping, enrichment, and technology activities in classrooms. These items are as follows:

- Work on assignments that have questions that you can correct on your own.
- Participate in a game that tests your knowledge of material you have learned.
- Interview adults about careers you are interested in pursuing.
- Work with a classmate to help her/him understand something that you already know.
- Play a computer game to learn new information.
- Work at a learning or interest center.
- Use a computer program to solve a problem.
- Participate in a group in which everyone has a different role and helps each other with their work.
- Use a computer program to learn new information.
- Use a computer program in which you answer questions on a topic you are studying.
- Role play the part of a famous person whose life interests you.

- Work with other students on a special project based on something that interests you.
- Exchange e-mail with someone about a topic of mutual interest.
- Watch a video with a narrator who explains new information.
- Act out the part of scientist, journalist, artist or some other professional person.
- Participate in a chat room or newsgroup over the Internet in which you discuss topics of interest.
- Have the teacher review what students should know.
- Watch a broadcast of a program to learn more on a topic you are studying in class.
- Work on activities that use the computer to help you learn information.
- Use a computer program that helps you review information you need to know for class.
- Use the Internet to find information to help you with a project you are working on for class.
- Participate in an interactive activity over the Internet.

Overall, we included 85 questions on the experimental version of the *Learning Styles Inventory*. Elementary school and middle school students in classrooms across the country completed the instrument. We analyzed the data collected and, based on the results, designed the *Learning Styles Inventory, Version III (LSI-III)*.

Sample Demographics

The sample was comprised of 2260 elementary and middle school students from 14 states. States represented included Connecticut, Georgia, Iowa, Idaho, Illinois, Indiana, Michigan, North Carolina, North Dakota, New Jersey, Ohio, Pennsylvania, Texas, and Virginia. Based on school placement, we separated the sample into two groups (1157 elementary school students and 1103 middle school students). We split each group into two stratified random samples based on grade, ethnicity, gender and placement. Tables 1-5 present the demographic information for elementary and middle school by subsample.

Table 1. Frequency Data for Students (Percentages by Grades)

School Placement	Grade	Sample 1 (*n*=1113)	Sample 2 (*n*=1147)
Elementary	2	8.5	10.4
	3	22.2	21.7
	4	33.6	37.4
	5	35.7	30.5
Middle	6	49.2	49.7
	7	26.8	25.6
	8	24.0	24.7

Table 2. Ethnicity of Students (Percentages by Sample)

	Elementary School		Middle School	
Ethnicity	Sample 1E (*n*=568)	Sample 2E (*n*=589)	Sample 1M (*n*=545)	Sample 2M (*n*=558)
African American	3.7	3.4	1.6	1.5
Asian American	1.9	2.5	1.3	.9
Hispanic/Latin American	4.2	5.4	.4	.5
Native American	.2	.7	1.7	.7
Caucasian	88.9	86.8	95.0	96.2
Other	1.1	1.2	0.0	.2

Table 3. Gender (Percentages by Sample)

	Elementary School		Middle School	
Gender	Sample 1E (*n*=568)	Sample 2E (*n*=589)	Sample 1M (*n*=545)	Sample 2M (*n*=558)
Female	52.5	48.2	50.1	52.6
Male	47.5	51.8	49.9	47.2
Undeclared				.2

Table 4. Class Placement (Percentages by Sample)

	Elementary School		Middle School	
Class Placement	Sample 1E (*n*=568)	Sample 2E (*n*=589)	Sample 1M (*n*=545)	Sample 2M (*n*=558)
General Education	49.5	47.7	73.2	69.9
Gifted Education	40.3	42.1	15.6	18.6
LD	5.1	3.4	7.9	7.3
Special Education	.9	2.2	.4	.4
Other (Title, etc.)	4.2	4.6	2.9	3.8

Table 5. Setting (Percentages by Sample)

	Elementary School		Middle School	
Setting	Sample 1E (*n*=568)	Sample 2E (*n*=589)	Sample 1M (*n*=545)	Sample 2M (*n*=558)
Urban	15.0	18.8	1.1	1.3
Suburban	39.6	39.7	64.2	59.4
Rural	45.4	41.5	34.7	39.1
Undeclared				.2

Construct Validity

Exploratory Factor Analysis

We conducted separate Exploratory Factor Analyses on Samples 1E and 1M using SPSS 10.0. We extracted factors using principal component analysis. Based on the theory used to develop items, we extracted nine components for each sample. After examining the VARIMAX rotated solution, we retained 7 factors for the elementary school sample and 8 factors for the middle school sample for final rotation and interpretation. In each case, the retained factors had sufficient numbers of items to adequately define the construct. Items were retained if they loaded at least .40 as recommended by Gable and Wolf (1993) on a single factor and did not "cross-load" on other factors. Following the Exploratory Factor Analysis, we reviewed the factor structure to check the conceptual practicality of the instruments. We removed several items because of redundancy in content. Sixty-one items remained on the scale for elementary school students and 68 items remained on the scale for middle school students. Table 6 lists the resulting factor names, and Tables 7 and 8 (see pages 16-19) present the items comprising each factor.

Table 6. Factors by Sample

Elementary School	Middle School
Direct Instruction	Direct Instruction
Instruction through Technology	Instruction through Technology
Simulations	Simulations
Independent Study	Independent Study
Projects	Projects
Peer Teaching	Peer Teaching
Drill & Recitation	N/A
N/A	Discussion
N/A	Teaching Games

Items Removed

Following the Exploratory Factor Analysis, we reviewed the factor structure to check the conceptual practicality of the instruments and removed several items because of redundancy in content. We removed other items when, as recommended by Gable and Wolf (1993), we applied a .40 limit on factor loading to the items. Removing these items did not adversely affect the Alpha Reliabilities. The removed items include:

Direct Instruction

- Learn new things by having the teacher present information in class. (Removed from both instruments.)
- Have the teacher call on individual students by name to answer questions. (Removed from middle school instrument only.)

Table 7. Items by Factor: Elementary School Sample (Exploratory Analysis)

Item	I	II	III	IV	V	VI	VII
Factor 1. Direct Instruction							
Hear the teacher present information to the class.	.73						
Listen as your teacher presents a lesson.	.30						
Listen to your teacher present various points of view on a subject.	.64						
Listen to your teacher explain new information.	.63						
Have the teacher lead a discussion on a new topic.	.57						
Have the teacher give specific instructions on how to do things.	.55						
Have the teacher review what students should know.	.52						
Learn new things by having the teacher present information in class.	.50						
Have the teacher make clear what is expected of the class.	.48						
Factor 2. Instruction through Technology							
Work on activities that use the computer to help you learn information.		.72					
Use a computer program that helps you review information you need to know for class.		.67					
Use a computer program to learn new information.		.67					
Use the Internet to find information to help you with a project for class.		.62					
Use a computer program in which you answer questions on a topic you are studying.		.60					
Participate in an interactive activity over the Internet.		.58					
Use a computer program to solve a problem.		.56					
Search sources in the library or on the Internet for information about a topic you are studying.		.52					
Participate in a chat room or newsgroup over the Internet in which you discuss topics of interest.		.47					
Watch a broadcast of a program to learn more on a topic you are studying in class.		.43					
Watch a video with a narrator who explains new information.		.41					
Play a computer game to learn new information.		.37					
Factor 3. Simulations							
Learn about possible careers by acting out the role of a job counselor and interviewing other students who are acting as job applicants.			.68				
Learn how government works by playing the role of an official working with a local citizen group.			.66				
Act out the part of scientist, journalist, artist or some other professional person.			.60				
Learn about the election process by playing the role of a member of a campaign team.			.60				
Role play the part of a famous person whose life interests you.			.59				
Learn about an event such as the signing of the Declaration of Independence by acting it out in class.			.58				
Interview adults about careers you are interested in pursuing.			.54				
Work with a committee to prepare a lesson to present to the class.			.45				

Continued on page 17.

Table 7 *continued.*

Item	I	II	III	IV	V	VI	VII
				Factor			
Factor 4. Independent Study							
Work by yourself to collect information on a topic of interest.				.72			
Work on your own to prepare material you will present to the class.				.66			
Work independently on a project you choose yourself.				.64			
Study on your own to learn new information.				.64			
Work on your own to study a topic you choose.				.63			
Work on your own to prepare material you can share with your class.				.62			
Plan a project to work on by yourself.				.60			
Go to the library by yourself to find more information about a topic.				.57			
Read a book to learn all about a topic you select.				.52			
Factor 5. Projects							
Work with other students in planning and completing a project.					.58		
Work with other students on a project the teacher suggests.					.57		
Work with other students to plan a project about a topic in class.					.56		
Work with other students on a project with little help from your teacher.					.56		
Discuss class material with a group of other students.					.50		
Work with other students on a special project based on something that interests you.					.50		
Go to the library with a committee to find information.					.46		
Prepare a written report with a committee.					.43		
Talk with other students in your class about a topic of interest.					.40		
Factor 6. Peer Teaching							
Have a friend help you learn difficult material.						.64	
Work in the back of your classroom with another student who will help you with schoolwork.						.58	
Learn new information from another student in your class.						.56	
Have a classmate teach you how to do something he or she does well.						.54	
Have a student in your grade work with you to review material for a test.						.53	
Factor 7. Drill & Recitation							
Have the teacher call on individual students by name to answer questions.							.62
Have the teacher ask questions to see what you have learned.							.55
Have a contest to see if your team can correctly answer questions about a topic you are studying in class.							.52
Have your teacher call on individual students to recite information that you have learned.							.52
Have a spelling bee with other students in your class.							.42
Be quizzed by your teacher to see if you understand a story you read.							.42
Do assignments in which you find out after each question whether your answer is correct.							.42
Work on assignments that have questions that you can correct on your own.							.38
Fill in the missing word to complete a sentence on an assignment.							.32

Table 8. Items by Factor: Middle School Sample (Exploratory Analysis)

Item	I	II	III	IV	V	VI	VII	VIII
Factor 1. Direct Instruction								
Listen as your teacher presents a lesson	.76							
Hear the teacher present information to the class.	.75							
Listen to your teacher present various points of view on a subject.	.73							
Listen to your teacher explain new information.	.72							
Have the teacher lead a discussion on a new topic.	.66							
Learn new things by having the teacher present information in class.	.66							
Have the teacher give specific instructions on how to do things.	.56							
Have the teacher ask questions to see what you have learned.	.54							
Have the teacher make clear what is expected of the class.	.53							
Have the teacher review what students should know.	.53							
Take notes as the teacher talks to the class.	.50							
Have the teacher call on individual students by name to answer questions.	.45							
Factor 2. Instruction through Technology								
Use a computer program to learn new information.		.85						
Use a computer program that helps you review information you need to know for class.		.81						
Work on activities that use the computer to help you learn information.		.79						
Use a computer program to solve a problem.		.78						
Use a computer program where you answer questions on a topic you are studying		.72						
Play a computer game to learn new information.		.72						
Use the Internet to find information to help you with a project for class.		.67						
Participate in an interactive activity over the Internet.		.64						
Search sources in the library or on the Internet for information about a topic you are studying.		.52						
Exchange e-mail with someone about a topic of mutual interest.		.51						
Participate in a chat room or newsgroup over the Internet in which you discuss topics of interest.		.46						
Watch a video with a narrator who explains new information.		.42						
Watch a broadcast of a program to learn more on a topic you are studying in class.		.41						
Factor 3. Simulations								
Learn how government works by playing the role of an official working with a local citizen group.			.72					
Role play the part of a famous person whose life interests you.			.71					
Act out the part of scientist, journalist, artist or some other professional person.			.71					
Learn about the election process by playing the role of a member of a campaign team.			.69					
Learn about an event such as the signing of the Declaration of Independence by acting it out in class.			.67					
Learn about possible careers by acting out the role of a job counselor and interviewing other students who are acting as job applicants.			.69					
Interview adults about careers you are interested in pursuing.			.51					
Work with a committee to prepare a lesson to present to the class.			.40					

Continued on page 19.

Table 8 *continued.*

Item	I	II	III	IV	V	VI	VII	VIII
Factor 4. Independent Study								
Work independently on a project you choose yourself.				.78				
Plan a project to work on by yourself.				.77				
Work on your own to prepare material you can share with your class.				.74				
Work on your own to study a topic you choose.				.73				
Work by yourself to collect information on a topic of interest.				.73				
Work on your own to prepare material you can share with your class.				.72				
Study on your own to learn new information.				.60				
Go to the library by yourself to find more information about a topic.				.49				
Read a book to learn all about a topic you select.				.44				
Factor 5. Projects								
Work with other students to plan a project about a topic in class.					.70			
Work with other students in planning and completing a project.					.65			
Work with other students on a project the teacher suggests.					.64			
Work with other students on a project with little help from your teacher.					.62			
Work with other students on a special project based on something that interests you.					.61			
Prepare a written report with a committee.					.51			
Discuss class material with a group of other students.					.49			
Participate in a group in which everyone has a different role and helps each other with their work.					.45			
Factor 6. Peer Teaching								
Have a classmate teach you how to do something he or she does well.						.70		
Learn new information from another student in your class.						.60		
Have a friend help you learn difficult material.						.54		
Work in the back of your classroom with another student who will help you with schoolwork.						.53		
Have a student in your grade work with you to review material for a test.						.51		
Work with a classmate to review homework assignments.						.49		
Factor 7. Discussion								
Hear the ideas of other students during a class discussion of an assigned topic.							.66	
Have other students present their ideas to the class.							.63	
Listen to classmates give their opinions on a subject.							.60	
Share ideas with other students during a class discussion.							.53	
Have a class discussion on a topic suggested by the teacher.							.46	
Talk with other students in your class about a topic of interest.							.44	
Factor 8. Teaching Games								
Practice vocabulary words by playing a word game.								.63
Have a spelling bee with other students in your class.								.62
Participate in a game that tests your knowledge of material you have learned.								.59
Play a game using flash cards in order to practice what you have learned.								.59
Have a contest to see if your team can correctly answer questions about a topic you are studying in class.								.54
Play a board game to help practice one of your school subjects.								.53

Instruction Through Technology

- Use a computer program in which you answer questions on a topic you are studying. (Removed from both instruments.)
- Search sources in the library or on the Internet for information about a topic you are studying. (Removed from both instruments.)
- Play a computer game to learn new information. (Removed from both instruments.)

Independent Study

- Work on your own to prepare material you can share with your class. (Removed from both instruments.)

Drill & Recitation

- Fill in the missing word to complete a sentence on an assignment.

Confirmatory Factor Analysis

In order to cross-validate results of the Exploratory Factor Analysis, we calculated separate Confirmatory Factor Analyses (CFA) for the second independent stratified random samples for the elementary and middle school instruments, respectively, using AMOS 4.0 (Arbuckle & Wothke, 1999). As the name implies, this analysis allowed the factor structure developed through the Exploratory Factor Analysis to be confirmed using an independent sample. Models reflected the results of the exploratory factor analysis. Tables 9 and 10 present the results of these analyses. As can be seen from the tables, all items load as expected on their respective scales. Table 11 presents fit indices for these analyses. Each set of fit indices points to the viability of these scales as adequately explaining the factorial structure of the scales. For all indices except RMSEA, values closer to 1.0 indicate a better fit. Byrne (1989) suggested that values > .90 indicate adequate fit. We would expect values of RMSEA to be small. Loehlin (1998) suggested that values <.05 indicate good fit. In either case, all values are very close to the ideal. The results of the Exploratory Factor Analyses were supported through use of a separate, independent sample with demographic characteristics very similar to the entire population.

Reliability

We computed Cronbach Alpha Reliability coefficients for each of the factors on both the elementary and middle school editions of the instrument. These reliabilities are based on the total sample for each level. All reliabilities are within accepted limits for this type of instrument, supporting the subscales as separate scores. These internal consistencies are based on the final forms of the factors (that is, after we removed items following the exploratory analysis). Tables 12 and 13 (see page 25) present the Alpha Reliability coefficients for the elementary and middle school instruments respectively,

As might be expected, reliabilities for the middle school instrument are somewhat higher than for

Table 9. Items by Factor: Elementary School Sample (Confirmatory Analysis)

Item	I	II	III	IV	V	VI	VII
Factor 1. Direct Instruction							
Hear the teacher present information to the class.	.79						
Listen as your teacher presents a lesson.	.74						
Listen to your teacher present various points of view on a subject.	.72						
Have the teacher lead a discussion on a new topic.	.65						
Have the teacher review what students should know.	.64						
Listen to your teacher explain new information.	.63						
Have the teacher give specific instructions on how to do things.	.62						
Have the teacher make clear what is expected of the class.	.53						
Factor 2. Instruction through Technology							
Work on activities that use the computer to help you learn information.		.73					
Use a computer program to learn new information.		.69					
Use a computer program that helps you review information you need to know for class.		.67					
Use the Internet to find information to help you with a project for class.		.67					
Participate in an interactive activity over the Internet.		.63					
Use a computer program to solve a problem.		.61					
Participate in a chat room or newsgroup over the Internet in which you discuss topics of interest.		.50					
Watch a video with a narrator who explains new information.		.50					
Watch a broadcast of a program to learn more on a topic you are studying in class.		.47					
Factor 3. Simulations							
Learn how government works by playing the role of an official working with a local citizen group.			.70				
Learn about possible careers by acting out the role of a job counselor and interviewing other students who are acting as job applicants.			.68				
Act out the part of scientist, journalist, artist or some other professional person.			.65				
Role play the part of a famous person whose life interests you.			.65				
Learn about the election process by playing the role of a member of a campaign team.			.62				
Work with a committee to prepare a lesson to present to the class.			.56				
Interview adults about careers you are interested in pursuing.			.52				
Learn about an event such as the signing of the Declaration of Independence by acting it out in class.			.40				
Factor 4. Independent Study							
Work on your own to study a topic you choose.				.70			
Work on your own to prepare material you will present to the class.				.66			
Plan a project to work on by yourself.				.65			
Work by yourself to collect information on a topic of interest.				.65			
Work independently on a project you choose yourself.				.65			
Study on your own to learn new information.				.53			
Go to the library by yourself to find more information about a topic.				.48			
Read a book to learn all about a topic you select.				.43			

Continued on page 22.

Table 9 *continued.*

Item	I	II	III	IV	V	VI	VII
				Factor			
Factor 5. Projects							
Work with other students in planning and completing a project.					.74		
Work with other students to plan a project about a topic in class.					.71		
Work with other students on a special project based on something that interests you.					.68		
Work with other students on a project the teacher suggests.					.59		
Prepare a written report with a committee.					.50		
Discuss class material with a group of other students.					.49		
Talk with other students in your class about a topic of interest.					.46		
Work with other students on a project with little help from your teacher.					.40		
Go to the library with a committee to find information.					.40		
Factor 6. Peer Teaching							
Work in the back of your classroom with another student who will help you with schoolwork.						.65	
Have a friend help you learn difficult material.						.61	
Have a classmate teach you how to do something he or she does well.						.62	
Have a student in your grade work with you to review material for a test.						.60	
Learn new information from another student in your class.						.54	
Factor 7. Drill & Recitation							
Have the teacher ask questions to see what you have learned.							.68
Have your teacher call on individual students to recite information that you have learned.							.64
Have the teacher call on individual students by name to answer questions.							.64
Be quizzed by your teacher to see if you understand a story you read.							.57
Do assignments in which you find out after each question whether your answer is correct.							.48
Have a spelling bee with other students in your class.							.44
Work on assignments that have questions that you can correct on your own.							.44
Fill in the missing word to complete a sentence on an assignment.							.40
Have a contest to see if your team can correctly answer questions about a topic you are studying in class.							.40

Table 10. Items by Factor: Middle School Sample (Confirmatory Analysis)

Item	I	II	III	IV	V	VI	VII	VIII
Factor 1. Direct Instruction								
Hear the teacher present information to the class.	.79							
Listen as your teacher presents a lesson.	.78							
Listen to your teacher present various points of view on a subject.	.74							
Listen to your teacher explain new information.	.71							
Have the teacher lead a discussion on a new topic.	.68							
Have the teacher ask questions to see what you have learned.	.59							
Have the teacher review what students should know.	.57							
Have the teacher make clear what is expected of the class.	.54							
Have the teacher give specific instructions on how to do things.	.52							
Take notes as the teacher talks to the class.	.55							
Factor 2. Instruction through Technology								
Use a computer program to learn new information.		.85						
Use a computer program that helps you review information you need to know for class.		.85						
Work on activities that use the computer to help you learn information.		.79						
Use a computer program to solve a problem.		.78						
Use the Internet to find information to help you with a project for class.		.69						
Participate in an interactive activity over the Internet.		.64						
Exchange e-mail with someone about a topic of mutual interest.		.54						
Participate in a chat room or newsgroup over the Internet in which you discuss topics of interest.		.46						
Watch a broadcast of a program to learn more on a topic you are studying in class.		.45						
Watch a video with a narrator who explains new information.		.40						
Factor 3. Simulations								
Act out the part of scientist, journalist, artist or some other professional person.			.76					
Role play the part of a famous person whose life interests you.			.75					
Learn how government works by playing the role of an official working with a local citizen group.			.71					
Learn about the election process by playing the role of a member of a campaign team.			.68					
Learn about an event such as the signing of the Declaration of Independence by acting it out in class.			.65					
Learn about possible careers by acting out the role of a job counselor and interviewing other students who are acting as job applicants.			.64					
Work with a committee to prepare a lesson to present to the class.			.50					
Interview adults about careers you are interested in pursuing.			.47					
Factor 4. Independent Study								
Work independently on a project you choose yourself.				.76				
Work on your own to study a topic you choose.				.75				
Work by yourself to collect information on a topic of interest.				.75				
Plan a project to work on by yourself.				.71				
Work on your own to prepare material you can share with your class.				.70				
Study on your own to learn new information.				.60				
Go to the library by yourself to find more information about a topic.				.51				
Read a book to learn all about a topic you select.				.47				

Continued on page 24.

Table 10 *continued.*

Item								
	I	II	III	IV	V	VI	VII	VIII
Factor 5. Projects								
Work with other students to plan a project about a topic in class.					.81			
Work with other students in planning and completing a project.					.73			
Work with other students on a project the teacher suggests.					.69			
Work with other students on a special project based on something that interests you.					.69			
Participate in a group in which everyone has a different role and helps each other with their work.					.60			
Discuss class material with a group of other students.					.57			
Work with other students on a project with a little help from your teacher.					.55			
Prepare a written report with a committee.					.47			
Factor 6. Peer Teaching								
Learn new information from another student in your class.						.70		
Have a student in your grade work with you to review material for a test.						.69		
Work in the back of your classroom with another student who will help you with schoolwork.						.66		
Work with a classmate to review homework assignments.						.62		
Have a classmate teach you how to do something he or she does well.						.62		
Have a friend help you learn difficult material.						.60		
Factor 7. Discussion								
Listen to classmates give their opinions on a subject.							.68	
Hear the ideas of other students during a class discussion of an assigned topic.							.67	
Share ideas with other students during a class discussion.							.65	
Have other students present their ideas to the class.							.54	
Talk with other students in your class about a topic of interest.							.52	
Have a class discussion on a topic suggested by the teacher.							.46	
Factor 8. Teaching Games								
Participate in a game that tests your knowledge of material you have learned.								.69
Play a game using flash cards in order to practice what you have learned.								.69
Practice vocabulary words by playing a word game.								.66
Play a board game to help practice one of your school subjects.								.59
Have a contest to see if your team can correctly answer questions about a topic you are studying in class.								.58
Have a spelling bee with other students in your class.								.54

Table 11. Fit Indices for Cross-Validation Samples

Fit Indices	NFI	IFI	TLI	CFI	PNFI	RMSEA
Elementary	.943	.939	.958	.961	.877	.06
Middle	.936	.957	.954	.957	.876	.058

Note. NFI = Bentler-Bonnett Normed Fit Index; IFI=Incremental Fit Index; TLI = Tucker-Lewis Coefficient; CFI = Comparative Fit Index; PNFI = Parsimony-adjusted NFI; RMSEA = Root Mean Square Error of Approximation.

Table 12. Alpha Reliability Coefficients: Elementary School Instrument

Factor	Reliability
Direct Instruction	.85
Instruction through Technology	.83
Simulations	.83
Independent Study	.80
Projects	.80
Drill & Recitation	.78
Peer Teaching	.74

Table 13. Alpha Reliability Coefficients: Middle School Instrument

Factor	Reliability
Direct Instruction	.89
Instruction through Technology	.88
Simulations	.86
Independent Study	.85
Projects	.84
Peer Teaching	.79
Teaching Games	.78
Discussion	.76

the elementary school instrument. Likewise, longer subscales have somewhat higher reliability coefficients than shorter scales.

Factor Descriptions

The Exploratory Factor Analysis for the elementary school sample yielded a 7-factor solution. The middle school sample yielded an 8-factor solution. This factor structure proved stable when exposed to the confirmatory analysis, and alpha reliabilities were adequate for an affective instrument of this type. As discussed earlier, the factors were conceptually similar across instruments and descriptions of each of the factors (with any minor differences by instrument described as necessary) follow:

Direct Instruction: Direct Instruction is comprised of items that involve direct teacher input. As the name implies, items on this factor include having the teacher present a lesson, explain new information, and present various viewpoints. The factor also contains items that include having the teacher give directions and lead discussions. The elementary school instrument contains 8 items as found on Table 14 (on page 26). The middle school instrument contains two additional items that describe events commonly found in middle school classrooms, but, according to the norm group, not in elementary classrooms. On Table 14, these items are followed by "middle school only."

Many of the items found on the Direct Instruction Factor come from the Lecture Factor on the original *LSI*. We changed the name to reflect the inclusion of items from other factors from the original version, especially Discussion and Programmed Instruction. It should be noted that items from Programmed Instruction also appear on the Drill & Recitation factor on the elementary school version of the instrument.

Instruction through Technology: Instruction through Technology contains 9 items on the elementary school instrument and 10 on the middle school instrument. The items on this factor are all related to the use of computers and other educational technology. Using computers to learn new information, review information, and participate in interactive activities are included on this factor. Activities that involve the Internet and communicating via e-mail and in chat rooms are also the subject of some items. In addition, video and television broadcasts are included in this factor. There is one additional item on the middle school instrument that relates to using e-mail, an activity that may not be available to most elementary school students. Table 15 contains the items on this factor.

Simulations: The Simulations factor contains 8 items that describe activities that contain role playing, acting, and real-world tasks. Students act as practicing professionals to learn first hand how to gather information and use that knowledge within simulation activities. Both instruments use the same items to define this factor (see Table 16).

Table 14. Items on Factor: Direct Instruction

Listen to your teacher explain new information.
Have the teacher give specific instructions on how to do things.
Have the teacher make clear what is expected of the class.
Listen as your teacher presents a lesson.
Have the teacher lead a discussion on a new topic.
Hear the teacher present information to the class.
Listen to your teacher present various points of view on a subject.
Have the teacher review what students should know.
Take notes as the teacher talks to the class. (middle school only)
Have the teacher ask questions to see what you have learned. (middle school only)

Table 15. Items on Factor: Instruction through Technology

Use a computer program to solve a problem.
Use a computer program to learn new information.
Watch a video with a narrator who explains new information.
Participate in a chat room or newsgroup over the Internet where you discuss topics of interest.
Watch a broadcast of a program to learn more on a topic you are studying in class.
Work on activities that use the computer to help you learn information.
Use a computer program that helps you review information you need to know for class.
Use the Internet to find information to help you with a project you are working on for class.
Participate in an interactive activity over the Internet.
Exhange e-mail with someone about a topic of mutual interest. (middle school only)

Table 16. Items on Factor: Simulations

Learn about an event such as the signing of the Declaration of Independence by acting it out in class.
Learn about the election process by playing the role of a member of a campaign team.
Learn about possible careers by acting out the role of a job counselor and interviewing other students who are acting as job applicants.
Learn how government works by playing the role of an official working with local citizen group.
Work with a committee to prepare a lesson to present to the class.
Interview adults about careers you are interested in pursuing.
Role play the part of a famous person whose life interests you.
Act out the part of scientist, journalist, artist, or some other professional person.

Independent Study: The Independent Study factor contains the same eight items on both instruments of the *LSI-III*. These items describe activities in which the student works alone. Items on this factor include studying alone, preparing projects, gathering information, and reading material chosen by the student or teacher. Table 17 lists these items.

Projects: The Projects factor contains 9 items on the elementary school instrument and 8 items on the middle school instrument (see Table 18). The items on this factor all describe groups of students working on various aspects of projects, and the majority of the items contain the word "project." There are also items that describe discussions, reports, and small group activities. The elementary school instrument contains two items not found on the Projects factor of the middle school instrument. One item, "Talk with other students in your class about a topic of interest," falls under the Discussion factor of the middle school instrument. The other differing item did not appear on any factor of the middle school instrument and may be measuring a preference for group activity rather than being an integral part of projects.

Peer Teaching: The Peer Teaching factor contains 5 items on the elementary school instrument and 6 items on the middle school instrument (see Table 19). The items on this factor describe activities in which students work together to learn information from each other. This factor includes items that describe activities such as "work[ing] with classmates and friends on new information or review material." The focus on the activities described in these items is on one student teaching another. The additional item found on the middle school instrument pertains to working on homework, an activity not common to elementary school students. Although a

Table 17. Items on Factor: Independent Study

Study on your own to learn new information.
Plan a project to work on by yourself.
Work on your own to prepare material you will present to the class.
Work on your own to study a topic you choose.
Work independently on a project you choose yourself.
Work by yourself to collect information on a topic of interest.
Go to the library by yourself to find more information about a topic.

Table 18. Items on Factor: Projects

Work with other students on a project with little help from your teacher.
Discuss class material with a group of other students.
Work with other students on a project the teacher suggests.
Work with other students to plan a project about a topic in class.
Work with other students in planning and completing a project.
Prepare a written report with a committee.
Work with other students on a special project based on something that interests you.
Go to the library with a committee to find information. (elementary school only)
Talk with other students in class about a topic of interest. (elementary school only)
Participate in a group in which everyone has a different role and helps each other with their work.
(middle school only)

certain amount of peer teaching occurs in cooperative learning situations, these situations should not be confused with the Peer Teaching factor on this instrument. For this instrument, Peer Teaching is defined as one student instructing another, an activity that may or may not occur within a cooperative learning situation. Furthermore, cooperative learning entails far more than peer instruction. For a closer approximation to a preference for cooperative learning situations, teachers should examine the student's preference for Projects in conjunction with the instructional practices used in the classroom, i.e. customary use of cooperative learning to accomplish group projects.

Drill & Recitation: This factor appears only on the elementary school instrument and contains 9 items similar to activities previously found on the Programmed Instruction factor of the original instrument. These items include being quizzed, called upon by the teacher, and doing assignments that ask the student for specific information. This factor does not appear on the middle school instrument because the activities are more indicative of an elementary school classroom, where students complete worksheets and are drilled by teachers on basic facts. Table 20 displays the items for this factor.

Discussion: This factor, which appears only on the middle school instrument, is characterized by 6 items that describe how students share their ideas and opinions (see Table 21). The items

Table 19. Items on Factor: Peer Teaching

Have a friend help you learn difficult material.
Have a classmate teach you how to do something he or she does well.
Learn new information from another student in your class.
Have a student in your grade work with you to review material for a test.
Work in the back of your classroom with another student who will help you with schoolwork.
Work with a classmate to review homework assignments. (middle school only)

Table 20. Items on Factor: Drill & Recitation

Be quizzed by your teacher to see if you understand a story you read.
Fill in the missing word to complete a sentence on an assignment.
Have a spelling bee with other students in your class.
Do assignments in which you find out after each question whether your answer is correct.
Have a contest to see if your team can correctly answer questions about a topic you are studying in class.
Work on assignments that have questions that you can correct on your own.
Have your teacher call on individual students to recite information that you have learned.
Have the teacher call on individual students by name to answer questions.
Have the teacher ask questions to see what you have learned.

Table 21. Items on Factor: Discussion

Listen to classmates give their opinions on a subject.
Hear ideas of other students during a class discussion of an assigned topic.
Share ideas with other students during a class discussion.
Have other students present their ideas to the class.
Talk with other students in your class about a topic of interest.
Have a class discussion on a topic suggested by the teacher.

describe either listening or talking while participating in a discussion, classroom activities common to the middle school experience, but rare in an elementary classroom. Discussion requires advanced thinking skills that may come with practice and maturity. Middle school students may also be responding to the social aspects implied by this factor.

Teaching Games: Teaching Games appears only on the middle school instrument and contains items that describe games and contests that allow students to show what they have learned. The games described in this factor are purposeful in nature and intended to support learning in some manner. The items also describe activities that may seem fun for students but actually represent the goal-directed nature of middle school learning. Middle school students may have responded more favorably to the gaming aspect of the learning activity than elementary students, whereas the elementary school students may not have truly understood the learning aspects of the games they may play in class. There is an implied acknowledgment of the maturity and metacognitive understanding in middle school students, which may be the true difference between them and their elementary school counterparts. Table 22 lists the items included in the Teaching Games factor.

Table 22. Items on Factor: Teaching Games

Participate in a game that tests your knowledge of material you have learned.
Play a game using flash cards in order to practice what you have learned.
Practice vocabulary words by playing a word game.
Play a board game to help practice one of your school subjects.
Have a contest to see if your team can correctly answer questions about a topic you are studying in class.
Have a spelling bee with other students in your class.

Scoring

Using data collected from the sample, we obtained means and standard deviations (see Table 23) and then converted them to t-scores for each subscale. T-scores ($x = 50$, $SD=10$) allow responses to be compared across factors that contain different numbers of items. Each t-score, therefore, corresponds to a total subscale score or range of scores depending on the factor (see Tables 24 and 25 on pages 30-31). In order to ease interpretation, we transformed the t-scores into converted scores of 1-10 (also found on Tables 24 and 25). These scores appear on the final instrument and in Table 26 (on page 31).

Table 23. Means and Standard Deviations for Raw Scores for Subscales

Factor	Elementary School Instrument		Middle School Instrument	
	Mean	SD	Mean	SD
Direct Instruction	23.1	6.1	22.9	8.1
Instruction through Technology	28.9	6.0	28.8	7.8
Simulation	24.0	6.2	21.7	6.8
Independent Study	22.8	6.2	17.7	6.8
Projects	27.1	5.9	22.5	5.9
Peer Teaching	14.7	4.0	16.5	4.4
Drill & Recitation	25.7	6.3	n/a	n/a
Discussion	n/a	n/a	16.4	4.1
Teaching Games	n/a	n/a	16.5	4.4

Table 24. Scoring Matrix: Elementary School Instrument

t-score	Direct Instruction	Instruction through Technology	Simulation	Independent Study	Projects	Peer Teaching	Drill & Recitation	Converted Scores
65	31-32	36	31-32	30-32	34-36	19-20	33-36	10
60	28-30	33-35	28-30	27-29	31-33	17-18	30-32	9
55	25-27	30-32	25-27	24-26	28-30	15-16	27-29	8
50	22-24	27-29	22-24	21-23	25-27	13-14	23-26	7
45	19-21	24-26	19-21	17-20	22-24	11-12	20-22	6
40	16-18	21-23	16-18	14-16	19-21	9-10	17-19	5
35	12-15	18-20	12-15	11-13	16-18	7-8	14-16	4
30	9-11	15-17	9-11	8-10	13-15	5-6	11-13	3
25	5-8	12-14	5-8	5-7	10-12	3-4	8-10	2
20	0-4	0-11	0-4	0-4	0-9	0-2	0-7	1

Table 25. Scoring Matrix: Middle School Instrument

t-score	Direct Instruction	Instruction through Technology	Simulation	Independent Study	Projects	Peer Teaching	Discussion	Teaching Games	Converted Scores
65	36-40	39-40	31-32	28-32	29-32	22-24	21-24	23-24	10
60	32-35	37-38	28-30	25-27	26-28	20-21	19-20	21-22	9
55	28-31	33-36	25-27	21-24	23-25	18-19	17-18	19-20	8
50	24-27	29-32	22-24	18-20	20-22	16-17	15-16	17-18	7
45	19-23	25-28	19-21	14-17	17-19	14-15	13-14	15-16	6
40	16-18	21-24	16-18	11-13	14-16	12-13	11-12	13-14	5
35	11-14	17-20	12-15	8-10	11-13	10-11	9-10	11-12	4
30	7-10	13-16	9-11	4-7	8-10	8-9	7-8	9-10	3
25	3-6	9-12	5-8	1-3	5-7	6-7	5-6	7-8	2
20	0-2	0-8	0-4	0-2	0-4	0-5	0-4	0-6	1

Table 26. Interpretation of Converted Scores

Converted Score	Preference Level
9-10	Very High
7-8	High
5-6	Average
3-4	Low
1-2	Very Low

REFERENCES

Arbuckle, J., & Wothke, W. (1999). *Amos 4.0*. Hillsdale, NJ: Lawrence Erlebaum.

Byrne, B. (1989). *A primer of LISREL: Basic applications and programming for confirmatory factor analytic models*. New York: Springer Verlag.

Loehlin, J. C. (1998). *Latent variable models* (3rd ed.). Hillsdale, NJ: Lawrence Erlbaum.

Gable, R. K., & Wolf, M. B. (1993). *Instrument development in the affective domain: Measuring attitudes and values in corporate and school settings* (2nd ed.). Boston: Kluwer Academic Publications.

Kettle, K. E., Renzulli, J. S., & Rizza, M. G. (1998). Products of mind: Exploring student preferences for product development using *My Way: An Expression Style Inventory. Gifted Child Quarterly, 42, 1,* 48-61.

Purcell, J. H., & Renzulli, J. S. (1998). *Total talent portfolio: A systematic plan to identify and nurture gifts and talents*. Mansfield Center, CT: Creative Learning Press.

Renzulli, J. S. (1977). *The Interest-A-Lyzer*. Mansfield Center, CT: Creative Learning Press.

Renzulli, J. S. (1997). *The Interest-A-Lyzer family of instruments: A manual for teachers*. Mansfield Center, CT: Creative Learning Press.

Renzulli, J. S., & Smith, L. H. (1978). *Learning styles inventory: A measure of student preference for instructional techniques*. Mansfield Center, CT: Creative Learning Press.

Renzulli, J. S., Smith, L. H., White, A. J., Callahan, C. M., Hartman, R. K., & Westberg, K. L. (2002). *Scales for Rating the Behavioral Characteristics of Superior Students—Revised Edition*. Mansfield Center, CT: Creative Learning Press.

APPENDIX A

Appendix A presents the theoretical rationale and underlying research that supports the useful-ness of information about student learning styles.

ABILITIES, INTERESTS, AND STYLES IN THE ACT OF LEARNING[1]

Year after year, government reports declare that our nation's schools are not adequately educating our children and preparing them for the rigors of the real world. In response, schools have increasingly turned to testing as a way to show that students are learning. While this reliance on testing placates the public cry for accountability, it does nothing to improve the education students receive. We believe that schools will fare much better if, instead of testing, teachers and administrators place the act of learning at the center of education (Renzulli, 1992), and the *Learning Styles Inventory* provides valuable information that can help schools reach that goal.

An act of learning takes place when three major components of instructional settings—a learner, a teacher, and the material to be learned (i.e., curriculum)—interact with one another in such a way as to produce the intellectual or artistic equivalent of spontaneous combustion (see Figure 1 (Renzulli, 1994, p. 19)). Although peer dynamics can also be a crucial factor in the learning process, these three components are the basic functional elements in classroom learning experiences.

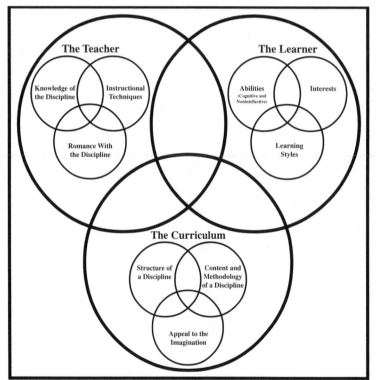

Figure 1. The ideal act of learning.

Each of these three major components of an act of learning has its own important subcomponents. For example, educators must look at each student's abilities, interest in the topic, and preferred styles of learning. With this knowledge, teachers can then present appropriate challenges matched to ability, work to enhance present interests or develop new interests, and present lessons to students in their preferred learning styles to improve motivation. Similarly, teachers must consider their roles in instructional techniques and the extent to which they have developed a "romance" with the material they are teaching. Finally, educators must examine the curriculum in terms of the structure of the discipline, the content and methodology of the discipline, and the extent to which the material appeals to the imagination of the learner. The intersecting circles in Figure 1 emphasize the *dynamic interactions* rather than linear relations between the components. This representation of the act of learning does

---

[1] Material in this appendix has been drawn from earlier *LSI* manuals and the following book chapter: Renzulli, J. S., & Dai, D. Y. (2001). Abilities, interests, and styles as aptitudes for learning: A person-situation interaction perspective. In Sternberg, R. J., & Zhang, L. (Eds.). *Perspectives on Thinking, Learning, and Cognitive Styles.* (pp. 23-46). London: Lawrence Earlbaum.

not assume equity among all components and subcomponents. The circles will vary in size from one learning situation to another, and variations will exist even within a single learning situation. Nonetheless, educators can optimize all acts of learning by organizing experiences that result in interplay among the three components. While educators must consider all three components, this appendix focuses on the learner and how educators can take advantage of the learner's abilities, interests, and learning styles.

Abilities as Developed and Developing Competencies

Although ability is universally considered crucial for successful learning, there are many theoretical accounts of the nature and origins of human abilities (Sternberg & Kaufman, 1998). Three traditions stand out as responsible for current thinking. Piaget and neo-Piagetian theorists argue that human abilities develop in a sequential fashion as a result of maturation and interaction with the environment (direct experience and social transmission) (Piaget, 1967; Case, 1985). A psychometric approach explains human abilities in terms of individual differences (Carroll, 1993; Guilford, 1959). And finally, cognitive psychology attempts to interpret abilities in terms of elementary processes (e.g., encoding and retrieval) and components (e.g., short-term and long-term memory, executive function) involved in learning and performance (Newell & Simon, 1972; Sternberg, 1985). Of the three traditions, the psychometric perspective on human abilities has had the most influence on the field of education. However, it may not hold up when evaluated using criteria from a learning/instruction perspective—that is, by looking at how well a theory explains factors that facilitate learning and how well a theory can be applied to instruction.

Take the example of IQ testing, a psychometric attempt to quantify ability: an age-normed test score is interpreted as a student's relative standing in a specific age population and an indicator of how well that student will do compared to age peers in the future. Problems occur when the score is interpreted as indicating some fixed ability, especially if interpreters infer that the ability is largely genetically determined (Herrnstein & Murray, 1994). Evidence is far from supporting this interpretation. First of all, the psychometric view of human abilities exaggerates individual differences found at one point in time and ignores the enormous developmental gains children make in cognitive competence as they grow up and are increasingly exposed to environmental stimuli (Lohman, 1993).

Second, many IQ tests that are supposed to measure natural ability are in fact measures of achievement (i.e., developed or developing competencies) (Lohman, 1993; Sternberg, 1998). Test sections on vocabulary, reading comprehension, and arithmetic problem solving typically found in IQ tests can be seen in part as measures of achievement. Thus researchers should not infer the causal precedence of natural ability from the correlation of IQ measures and academic achievement. Since there has been no reliable and valid measure of individual differences in pure natural abilities, all ability tests should be treated as measures of developed or developing competencies (Anastasi, 1980; Sternberg, 1998).

Third, the claim of heritability of intelligence is based heavily on genetic studies of twins that consistently found heritability estimates to be somewhere between .50 to .78. In other words, half or more than half of the total variance in IQ scores is accounted for by genetic factors (Plomin & Petrill, 1997). While this may seem strong evidence, there remains a large portion of variance unexplained by genetic factors. Furthermore, remarkable increases in IQ scores found over the generations (Flynn, 1994, 1999) have led many researchers to look into various environmental factors (such as better nutrition, more parental attention, and increased schooling) for answers (see Sternberg & Kaufman, 1998, for a review). Increasing evidence also suggests that intelligence may have nonintellective origins. For example, the quality of interaction between infants and their caregivers was found to be related to differences in cognitive abilities two years later (Lewis, 1989). Other "nonintellective" factors, such as temperaments (e.g., persistence, activity, and distractibility; see Thomas & Chess, 1977), may also contribute to (or retard) the development of cognitive abilities.

In addition to asking how adequate the psychometric view of human abilities is in explaining student learning and achievement, researchers can also look at how useful this approach is to instruction. Though the psychometric view may help educators identify different ranges of ability or achievement for appropriate, differentiated services, IQ test scores themselves do not help teachers determine the readiness of a student for a specific set of curricula. In other words, the diagnostic utility of psychometric tests of cognitive abilities is limited. Even worse, the results of these tests may send the wrong message to teachers and students that some students are fundamentally flawed and limited in their intellectual capacity simply because they have low scores. As Sternberg (1998) argued, no test of abilities can specify the limit of a student's learning potential. Moreover, since the psychometric perspective conveys the message that ability is fixed and innate, educators may completely lose sight of one of the most important goals of education—developing students' abilities.

If the psychometric perspective of human abilities does not provide adequate explanations for successful learning, what would be an alternative? A more promising approach is to view measured or observed abilities of the student from a developmental perspective—that is, as developed and developing competencies. As developed competencies, they tell educators about a student's current level of abilities. As developing competencies, they inform educators about how they may design their instruction to further advance these competencies. While a student's cognitive abilities may not be as malleable at the age of 16 as they were at the age of 8, most learning difficulties that most students encounter are remediable. Many individual differences in the ease and pace of learning previously believed to be due to deficits in general ability can now be more accurately diagnosed, and teachers can make changes in their curriculum design and instruction that take into account these differences.

Howard Gardner's (1983) theory of multiple intelligences and Robert Sternberg's (1985) triarchic theory of human intelligence have changed the narrow view of intelligence and human ability as unitary and being manifested only in psychometric testing. They point out that each individual is equipped with a unique set of potentials and strengths. The issue is not who has the ability and who does not, but how to capitalize on and develop these potentials and strengths.

One way teachers can help students develop their abilities is by first assessing student strengths through standardized test scores, curriculum-based assessments, and product evaluation. These assessments indicate students' prior knowledge in a particular area, and teachers can then give students credit for that prior knowledge and allow students time for developing additional abilities. A teaching strategy such as curriculum compacting gives the student credit for what he or she already knows and provides opportunities for him or her to use their time to develop other abilities.

However, abilities are not the only thing important for successful learning. The preoccupation with ability or intelligence has led to a disregard for other important characteristics in students that are responsible for successful learning. Educators must also consider interests as they may be the most important condition that promote active cognitive engagement in learning tasks.

Using Interests to Facilitate Learning

An interest is one of those psychological phenomena easily understood in everyday language, but difficult to define scientifically. We define interest as an affective leaning toward certain objects, phenomena, topics, or activities, and this definition includes three essential features. First, interests are directive or conative; they display a tendency to move or be drawn toward a certain direction (Snow, 1992). Second, all interests have certain degrees of intensity. Interests could be indicated by behaviors to deeply engage oneself in a purposeful activity or by affective reaction and arousal such as excitement and enjoyment when involved with a specific object or activity. Third, interests are dynamic; they occur or manifest themselves in a flow of events involving person-object interactions and relations, and the nature of a specific interest can only be understood in that dynamic person-object relation (Prenzel, 1992).

Most pertinent to learning are the questions of what makes a learner interested in a domain or a topic to the extent that it prompts a desire to learn more and what sustains and develops that interest. Piaget viewed interests as sine quo non for development. His theory of disequilibration and development of new cognitive structures is predicated on the assumption that there is an inherent tendency in children toward constructing knowledge and understanding that is consistent with their perceptual experiences of the world. To him, epistemic curiosity—a spontaneous interest in exploring the world outside and inside, particularly when reality is at variance with their expectations—is the defining feature of a developing child. This characteristic is evident when children keep asking adults "why" about a myriad of things. Furthermore, studies on human curiosity have led some researchers to the conclusion that curiosity results from the cognitive deprivation one encounters when objects and phenomena are beyond full comprehension (Loewenstein, 1994).

From a motivational rather than cognitive perspective, several American psychologists postulated that human beings have an innate tendency toward mastery of the environment (effectance motivation) (White, 1959), that experiences of personal causation are intrinsically rewarding (deCharms, 1968), and that feelings of personal agency, efficacy, and control are fundamental to human motivation (Bandura, 1977, 1986, 1997). A rudimentary form of this competence motivation can be observed in children's play. Manipulating toys is intrinsically pleasurable because it gives the child a sense of control, power, and competence as the child overcomes challenges and experiences successful mastery. Thus, interest is symptomatic of these internal forces of motivation and successful control of aspects of the environment.

However, the question remains: why are some children more interested in schoolwork than others, and why do some children display different interest patterns and different degrees of the same interest? The answers lie in the reality that there are many constraints affecting interest development. Careful analysis of these constraints will enable educators to develop instructional strategies to facilitate and unleash intrinsic motivation in the child to learn.

Social-cultural constraints. Not all children's interests are endorsed by parents, teachers, or peers. Those interests that deviate from societal norms tend to be inhibited or repressed. If a family, school, peer group, or society as a whole pushes for excellence in sports and has high tolerance for mediocrity in academics, children's interests are more likely to gravitate toward sports than academics (Tannenbaum, 1962). On the other hand, if the school places so much emphasis on academic achievement that some children feel anxious or insecure, interest in academics is likely to suffer. However, if school staffs make a coordinated effort to promote classrooms as communities of learners aimed at high-end learning (Brown, 1997), interests in school subjects are more likely to develop.

Opportunity structure constraints. These constraints refer to the fact that at a given time, each individual only has limited exposure or access to certain aspects of civilization, culture, and human endeavor. Doctors' families tend to produce doctors and musicians' families are more likely to produce musicians. In short, the resources available to children profoundly influences what types of interest they will develop over time. This phenomenon has important ramifications for school children who usually don't have choice and control over what is available to them. Schools, which are supposed to enlighten children's minds, very often do not provide the adequate intellectual stimuli and do not transform the curricula into exciting experiences of encountering new ideas, knowledge, and puzzles (Phenix, 1987). Without this necessary stimuli, schools will not open doors of opportunity to children; students cannot develop interests in ideas or activities to which they have not been exposed.

Knowledge constraints. Related to opportunity structure constraints are knowledge constraints. Interest in a domain is always based on some experience and understanding of that domain, even though the understanding may be vague and intuitive or even naïve. Interests could be superficial or deep depending on levels of understanding and knowledge. As knowledge of a domain or subject develops, a student's interest is also likely to undergo transformations from attending to those surface features to focusing on structural features of the domain (Alexander, Kulikowich, & Schulze, 1994). Thus, development of a deep, intrinsic interest in a domain, school subject, or topic takes a prolonged period of deep involvement in that domain, subject, or topic. This process could be disrupted by various situational circumstances, such as environmental restrictions and competing priorities (e.g., taking time away from the regular curriculum to prepare students for state-wide, grade-level testing), and/or personal factors, such as distractibility and lack of persistence.

Temperament and personality constraints. Just as nonintellective personal factors could affect the development of abilities, temperament and personality factors could also facilitate or hinder the development of interest. Although developmental potential is present for all children, some children are more intellectually excitable than others, and some are more persistent in pursuing an interest than others. This persistence may partly derive from two main personal factors. One is *achievement motivation*—the tendency to push one's limits and maximize satisfaction from mastery and success (Atkinson, 1957; Bandura, 1986). The other is *self-regulation*—self-generated thoughts, feelings, and actions that are designed systematically toward achieving a goal (Zimmerman, 1990; Kuhl, 1985). Metaphorically, the former can be seen as fuel or the driving force, while the latter can be seen as the engine that makes achievement work properly. Thus, it is misleading to conceive interest development as effortless. It takes dedicated effort and volition.

Ability constraints. For whatever reasons—genetic or environmental—there are individual differences in the ability to learn and perform a specific task that involves certain degrees of skill and expertise. Consciously or subconsciously, individuals tend to gravitate toward those domains or activities they perceive as their strengths (Deci, 1992). Thus, real ability levels or self-perceptions of abilities constrain how interested a person is or will be in a specific task, topic, or domain. Evidence suggests that students regulate their academic interest based on their self-perceptions of competence in a subject (Mac Iver, Stipek, & Daniels, 1991; Deci, 1992; Harter, 1992). At the same time, there is evidence that emergence of high intellectual abilities in childhood is associated with intrinsic interests across academic subjects (Gottfried & Gottfried, 1996). However, these two findings suggest nothing about *developing* interests and abilities. Research shows that children with learning difficulties and low interest in math became more interested in math when they saw themselves making progress (Bandura & Schunk, 1981). Consistent with the theory of competence motivation, experience of even moderate success increases interest.

Developmental constraints. If Piaget is correct, most children's comprehension of abstract topics is very limited until they reach age 11 or 12. In most cases, it is not until adolescence that individuals can mentally manipulate various possibilities and develop interests in purely theoretical issues such as origins of the universe or the microstructure of physical substance. Likewise, without certain levels of social-emotional maturity and experiences, sympathetic understanding of characters such as Hamlet or Othello cannot be achieved, let alone a genuine interest in tragedy as a genre. Although children's cognitive competence was somewhat underestimated by earlier pioneering psychologists such as Piaget, developmental constraints do set limits to what kinds of interests are most likely to develop and how these interests can be facilitated.

To summarize, interests are an important part of the act of learning, and there are social, personal, and developmental factors that constrain interest development. Some of these constraints are part of the external world that comes to influence the child. Others are internal, such as ability and temperamental constraints (see Dai, Moon, & Feldhusen, 1998). Addressing these constraints properly through differentiated curricula and instruction will facilitate students' cultivation of academic interests.

Using an information interest assessment tool such as the *Interest-A-Lyzer* (Renzullli, 1997, 1997) provides teachers with information that can be used to plan learning activities for students to explore interests. For example, if students indicate interest in journalism on their *Interest-A-Lyzers*, the teacher might plan a series of history assignments that ask students to write about particular historical events as if they were journalists at the time. Teachers can also offer opportunities for students to develop interests by providing a variety of exploratory activities. For example, students might take a field trip to a museum, visit with a guest speaker from another country, or participate in an interview of an author on the web. Building educational experiences around student's interests is undoubtedly one of the most powerful ways to improve student engagement and performance. These exploratory activities introduce new ideas and experiences to students and open up the range of possible interests.

Reaching Students through Learning Styles

Style, according to Guild and Garger (1985), is a combination of cognition, conceptualizations, affect, and behavior. These factors, alone and in combination, account for differences in human beings. Style was first used as a psychological term referring to differences in personality, perception, and cognition. Educators use the term to account for differences in learning, and many researchers have studied the concept of style and have constructed instruments that claim to identify it. Instruments such as the *Myers-Briggs Type Indicator* (Myers & Briggs, 1976) and the *Style Delineator* (Gregorc, 1982) address personality aspects of style. Other instruments such as the *Learning Style Inventory* (Dunn, Dunn, & Price, 1978), the *4MAT System* (McCarthy, 1980, 1990), and the *Learning Styles Inventory* (Renzulli & Smith, 1978) identify the educational implications of style and learning in school.

Early studies in this area have suggested that the most important characteristics in which students differ are their styles of learning (Hunt, 1971; Joyce & Weil, 1972; Pascal, 1971; Rosenberg, 1968; Tanner & Lindgren, 1971; Vinton, 1968). To optimize learning and facilitate the learning process, knowledge of a student's preferred style of learning can provide vital information that educators can apply to all three components of the act of learning—the learner, the teacher, and the curriculum. For example, teachers who have identified the learning preferences of their students can vary instruction to accommodate these preferences. In understanding and respecting students' learning style preferences, teachers validate the students as learners. Concurrently, the student gains insight into her or his own learning preferences that can provide direction for self-regulated learning. Finally, from a process point of view, understanding learning preferences can help educators differentiate the curriculum: educators can modify both curriculum implementation and expected outcomes according to the learning preferences of the students.

One of the major assumptions underlying the model presented earlier in Figure 1 is that in order for a real act of learning to take place, educators must take into consideration how the child would like to pursue a particular activity as well as the rate of learning and the child's preference for a certain topic. Consider the following example: In a classroom in which the teacher decides the mode of instruction, students are forced to adapt to the method the teacher has chosen. However, allowing a child some latitude in shaping his or her own learning environment may provide positive results in learning because it allows the child to spend more time concentrating on the learning task rather than adapting to an incongruent learning situation. Additionally, when a student works within a self-selected environment, he or she is likely to follow through with an activity for the sake of discovering and learning more, not merely fulfilling requirements. This assumption does not imply that complete freedom of choice should exist for all educational activities. On the contrary, certain basic skill areas are more appropriately taught through one approach rather than another. The number of such cases, however, is more limited than current practices would suggest, and educators should not be timid about taking additional steps toward individualizing instruction based on learning styles.

A large number of research studies provide support for a concept about learning that educators have known about and talked about for years—that students usually learn more easily and enjoyably when they are taught in a manner that is consistent with their preferred style of learning. Preferences may vary within the individual according to content area and interest in certain topics, a reality that may cause some teachers to narrow their teaching styles for simplicity's sake. However, if they do not make some effort to identify and accommodate these preferences, they will lose valuable opportunities for improving both student achievement and enjoyment for learning. As Torrance (1965) has pointed out, "alert teachers have always been aware of the fact that when they change their method of teaching, certain children who had appeared to be slow learners or even non-learners become outstanding achievers" (p. 253).

Matching Students to Learning Environments

Because the teacher and curriculum dimensions illustrated in Figure 1 take into account the teaching methods used to facilitate learning and the objectives that students are expected to achieve, they are primarily responsible for the creation of learning environments. A large number of studies have examined how matching students with various learning environments affects cognitive outcomes and student satisfaction with different types of educational processes. These studies fall into two general classifications: those studies dealing with the discrepancy or congruence between the personality characteristics of teachers and students and those studies dealing with the discrepancy or congruence between students and the instructional environment provided by teachers. The discussion that follows will deal only with those studies that fall into the second category because they are more relevant to the research and development underlying the *LSI* (a comprehensive review of studies falling into the first category can be found in Smith, 1976).

The studies that relate most directly to the *LSI* involve matching students to different instructional strategies based upon students' own assessments of their needs and preferences. The first of these studies was carried out by James (1962) who addressed the question: Do individuals who are given learning material by the mode of their preference actually learn better than those individuals who are given the material in a mode unlike their choice (p. 44)? James asked over 500 basic airmen to indicate whether they preferred a reading presentation in which written material would be learned independently or a lecture presentation. The 500 men were then grouped according to their preferred mode, and each group was then randomly divided into two groups of equal size, with one group receiving a written presentation and the other receiving a tape-recorded lecture over a public address system. At the end of the course, all participants received a 30-item multiple-choice test. Results indicated a significant interaction (p .05) between the subject's expressed choice and mode of presenting the material to be learned. In other words, there was an overall significant difference in scores on the criterion measure between students who received learning material in the preferred versus nonpreferred mode of instruction.

Pascal (1971) carried out a second study dealing with student self-matching. Pascal examined the educational effects of matching instructional strategies to students' learning style preferences with a sample of 185 university students enrolled in an undergraduate course in psychology. These students received a brief description of three instructional options—lecture, lecture and discussion, and independent study—and were asked to rank their preference for each instructional option. About one-half of these students were randomly assigned to the option that they listed as their first choice. The remaining students were randomly placed in either their second or third choice option. Results indicated that students allowed to learn through their preferred learning style showed a more positive attitude toward psychology than did students who did not receive their first choice. No differences were found with respect to grades or course evaluations. Several other outcomes, however, are noteworthy. Pascal found that nonpreferred independent study students rated the course more difficult and anxiety-producing (p -<.01) than did students who preferred this option. Students also reported being in favor of having options (93.5 percent positive) and generally felt that options provided them with "freedom and individualization" (91.6 percent positive). Thus, learning style matching not only gave students an opportunity to become involved in planning their educational experiences, but also resulted in enhancing students' attitude toward the subject matter.

Stahl and Kuhn (1995) found that understanding student learning styles alone was not sufficient to influence learning in reading. Only when instruction was altered to meet the needs of the students did change occur. In addition, matching instructional techniques to student styles was among the contributing factors that lead to improved motivation for elementary and middle school students according to Ellington, Long, and McCullough (1997). Campbell (1990) studied a group of sixth grade students who received instruction based on learning styles. Outcomes for the project included improved work habits and more positive classroom attitudes and behaviors by the students.

Ast (1988) further described the implications of correlating student learning styles with teaching styles and the influence of the curriculum, arguing that learning is based on internal and external factors that combine to influence the development of personality and motivation. Students who learn within their learning style tend to have higher achievement, are more interested, and are motivated to learn. Teachers, according to Ast, are the key to insuring that there is a match between curricular events and student learning styles by either providing students with experiences that match styles or helping students adapt to the environment.

Overall, the findings from these investigations suggest that an effort to match teaching strategies to students' learning style preferences may be beneficial. The results of a validation study carried out on the first edition of the *LSI* that examined the effectiveness of self-matching with a sample of school-age children (Renzulli & Smith, 1984) supports this conclusion.

Matching Instructional Techniques to Learning Styles

Although some teachers instinctively adjust their instructional techniques to the learning style preferences of individual students, the basis for these adaptations is usually informal (Cronbach, 1967; Lesser, 1971). The teacher may obtain cues during his or her interaction with students and then proceed on these impressions to alter instructional style. As well intentioned as these teachers may be, Cronbach (1967) has suggested that intuitive adaptations will often be inefficient and may occasionally be harmful. Lesser (1971, p. 3) contends that intuition alone "seems both insufficient to the magnitude of the present demands [of education] and poorly suited to building cumulative knowledge about instruction." Instead, educators need a more explicit, systematic method of assessing learning style preferences that can supplement their intuitive understanding of students. The *LSI-III* is an attempt to fulfill this need by providing a more complete characterization of the learner. Teachers can then apply the abundance of alternative teaching materials more effectively, resulting in a better response by the individual student to his or her learning environment.

In addition, the *LSI-III* points out the variety of learning style preferences within a classroom so that teachers may make better use of the wide array of instructional approaches that are available to them. Since there is no one fool-proof, multipurpose teaching strategy, providing a "cafeteria of alternatives" within the classroom should enable the teacher to reach more children (Joyce & Weil, 1972) and diminish the problem of "boring some and bewildering others" (McNamee, 1971). As Joyce and Hodges (1966) suggest, "a teacher who can purposefully exhibit a wide range of teaching styles is potentially able to accomplish more than a teacher whose repertoire is relatively limited" (p. 409). Improving the quality of instruction may thus be tied to increasing the variety of instructional techniques used in the classroom. The *LSI-III* will help direct the teacher's attention to the strategies that are most useful for particular subgroups of students.

Finally, the research underlying the development of the *LSI-III* may also help dispel what Tanner and Lindgren (1971) consider a common misconception in education: that common goals—the need for all students to master a particular body of knowledge— necessarily require common instruction. As Tanner and Lindgren (1971) suggest, "The theme that each learner will have the same basic understanding of a discipline may act as a psychological deterrent to varying the teaching method in accordance with the needs of the individual learner" (p. 151). By identifying individual student's learning style preferences, it is possible that more teachers will realize that a variety of paths can and need be provided to reach common goals.

Creating Spontaneous Combustion in the Classroom

Based on more than twenty years of field research, the Schoolwide Enrichment Model (Renzulli & Reis, 1985, 1997) was designed to bring about positive changes in students with diverse backgrounds and profiles of abilities, interests, and styles and to make the act of learning (as described earlier in Figure 1) the primary focus in the classroom. The Schoolwide Enrichment Model presents a set of specific strategies for increasing student effort, enjoyment, and performance and for integrating a broad range of advanced learning experiences and high-order thinking skills into any curricular area, course of study, and pattern of school organization. Central to this plan is the effort to encourage and facilitate the demonstration and development of individual learners' interests and talents.

Educators achieve this goal by employing three specific strategies. First, they must institute instructional procedures and programming that provide all students with a broad range of exploratory experiences (e.g., guest speakers, field trips, and interest centers) and expose students to a variety of exciting topics, ideas, and fields of knowledge not ordinarily covered in the regular curriculum. Students' responses to these experiences (interest level) indicate whether they should pursue more advanced, follow-up activities. For example, a guest speaker talking about pollution problems in the community may engage the curiosity of some students. As a result, these interested students may form an enrichment cluster in order to carry out a research project on the conditions of local rivers. As part of the process, the group relies on each member's strengths and each member becomes a specialist within the group. Such activities not only make learning personally meaningful and intrinsically rewarding, they also facilitate critical and creative thinking in a way that cannot be achieved by didactic instruction and textbook learning. Research has shown that students who participated in these exploratory activities identified more interests than comparable students who did not (Stednitz, 1985) and that students who were involved in more productive-creative activities had higher self-efficacy with regard to creative productivity (Starko, 1986).

Second, a strength assessment guide called *The Total Talent Portfolio* (Purcell & Renzulli, 1998) helps promote students' self-awareness and forethought as well as assessment of their strengths, interests, and cognitive/learning styles on a regular basis. It contains the student's self-ratings; teachers' observations, suggestions, and recommendations; the student's short-term and long-term goals; written products; and documentation of the student's activities in and outside of school relevant to the development of interests and talents. Students have control over the folder and its contents as they formulate and refine criteria to determine which products they will include in the portfolio. The TTP changes the way students perceive evaluation; instead of focusing on who is doing better than whom in a class, students focus on how they can capitalize on their strengths while avoiding or compensating for their weaknesses, an essential ingredient of successful intelligence (Sternberg, 1998). With the TTP in hand, students are more mindful of what particularly fascinates them (interests), what is easy or difficult for them (abilities), what comes naturally for them (styles), what they hope to achieve (goals), and how far they have gone (self-monitoring), a kind of metacognition highly valuable for self-directed and self-regulated learning (see Schunk & Zimmerman, 1994). (Appendix B presents a more thorough discussion of the TTP.)

Third, assessment becomes an integral part of instruction and learning because making appropriate instructional interventions depends on this assessment information. Prior to instruction, educators gather information about a student's abilities, interests, and styles, including test scores, grades, and self-ratings. This information is called *status information* and it helps teachers understand a student's present abilities, interests and learning styles. During instruction, teachers obtain further information through direct observations in regular classrooms or during enrichment activities. Some new interests or strengths may emerge in the process. These observations form *action information*—information that helps educators make decisions about appropriate instructional arrangements and activities for particular students. For example, for those students who are clearly underchallenged by the regular curricular materials, teachers may decide to compact the curriculum (Reis, Burns, & Renzulli, 1992) (condense the material into fewer lessons) so that students can spend time on more advanced, "high-end" learning tasks that are commensurate with the students' level of knowledge and skills.

Two principles underlie this instructional sequence or design. First, assessment is an ongoing, dynamic process and multidimensional in nature. Traditional standardized tests still serve as one of many indicators of students' strengths. However, no single normative rank score can be a substitute for a sound judgment based on a careful analysis and synthesis of multiple sources and dimensions of information. Second, educators should differentiate instruction as much and as frequently as possible in response to emergent characteristics of the learner, be it a newly found passion for a topic or difficulty understanding a mathematical concept. Differentiating curricula and instructional activities does not mean privileged treatments for high-achieving students and lower standards for low-achieving students. Rather, it addresses the needs of each individual student in the act of learning and promotes positive experiences crucial for successful learning, talent development, and personal growth.

Conclusion

At the beginning of a new century, the dilemma of how to reform schools looms large. With the increasing diversity of student populations, imposing uniform standards "from the top down" is a tough sell. Suggestions for more external regulation such as increasing "high-stakes testing" may appeal to the public's desire for accountability, but such measures may only create an illusion of improved achievement. The reality is that increased pressure on schools to expand the use of compensatory learning models contribute only to the "dumbing down" of curriculum and lowering of the standards. We suggest a different approach that is designed to develop each child's talents and strengths. We are less concerned with who has the highest test scores and more with providing the best educational experiences to any given child by taking into account factors such as interests and learning styles. We are not as concerned with raising test scores as with increasing students' intrinsic motivation to learn and improving self-direction and self-regulation. Academic achievement is an important part of the overall educational goal, but a focus on capitalizing on and developing each child's strengths and talents places the need for improved academic achievement into a larger perspective. What has made our nation great and our society productive is the manifestation of talent development at all levels and aspects of human activity. From the creators and inventors of new ideas, products, and art forms to the vast array of people who manufacture, advertise, and market these creations that enrich our lives, there are levels of excellence and quality that contribute to our standard of living and way of life. Our vision of a school for talent development grows out of the belief that everyone has an important role to play in the improvement of society and that everyone's role can be enhanced if schools provide all students with the opportunities, resources, and encouragement to develop their talents as fully as possible. From this point of view, the diversity of our student population is a strength rather than a weakness. In short, we believe first that the strengths of our culture lie in its emphasis on individuality and responsibility. Second, learning is an active, constructive, personally meaningful activity that not only takes cognitive resources but entails affect and motivation. Third, each child has inner resources which, when properly cultivated and channeled, can produce the most desirable educational outcomes we can ever imagine. It is our responsibility and our greatest challenge to bring the best out of each child.

REFERENCES

Alexander, P. A., Kulikowich, J. M., & Schulze, S. K. (1994). How subject-matter knowledge affects recall and interest. *American Educational Research Journal, 31*, 313-337.

Anastasi, A. (1980). Abilities and the measurement of achievement. In W. B. Schrader (Ed.), *Measuring achievement: Progress over a decade* (pp. 1-10). San Francisco: Jossey-Bass.

Ast, H. J. (1988, November). *Learning styles: Implications for curriculum and instruction.* Paper presented at the Alberta Association for Adult Literacy Conference, Calgary, Alberta. (ERIC Reproduction Service ED302280)

Atkinson, J. W. (1957). Motivational determinants of risk taking behavior. *Psychological Review, 64,* 359-372.

Bandura, A. (1977). Self-efficacy: Toward a unifying theory of behavioral change. *Psychological Review, 84*, 191-215.

Bandura, A. (1986). *Social foundations of thought and action: A social cognitive theory.* Englewood Cliffs, NJ: Prentice Hall.

Bandura, A. (1997). *Self-efficacy: The exercise of control.* New York: W. H. Freeman.

Bandura, A., & Schunk, D. H. (1981). Cultivating competence, self-efficacy, and intrinsic interest through proximal self-motivation. *Journal of Personality and Social Psychology, 41*, 586-598.

Barbe, W. B., & Swassing, R. H. (1979). *Teaching through modality strengths: Concept and practices.* Columbus, OH: Zaner-Bloser, Inc.

Brown, A. (1997). Transforming schools into communities of thinking and learning about serious matters. *American Psychologist, 52*, 399-413.

Campbell, L. J. (1990). *Using individual learning style inventories and group teaching methods in a sixth grade classroom.* Nova University. (ERIC Reproduction Service ED336687)

Carroll, J. B. (1993). *Human cognitive abilities: A survey of factor-analytic studies.* New York: Cambridge University Press.

Case, R. (1985). *Intellectual development: Birth to adulthood.* Orlando, FL: Academic Press.

Cronbach, L. J. (1967). How can instruction be adapted to individual differences? In R. M. Gagne (Ed.), *Learning and individual differences.* Columbus, OH: Merril Books.

Dai, D. Y., Moon, S. M., & Feldhusen, J. F. (1998). Achievement motivation and gifted students: A social cognitive perspective. *Educational Psychologist, 33*, 45-63.

deCharms, R. (1968). *Personal causation: The internal affective determinants of behavior.* New York: Academic Press.

Deci, E. L. (1992). The relation of interest to the motivation of behavior: A self-determination theory perspective. In K. A. Renninger, S. Hidi, & A. Krapp (Eds.), *The role of interest in learning and development* (pp. 43-70). Hillsdale, NJ: Lawrence Erlbaum Associates.

Dunn, R., Dunn, K., & Price, G. E. (1978). *Learning style inventory.* Lawrence, KS: Price Systems.

Ellington, W. E., Long, E. A., & McCullough, K. L. (1997). Improving student motivation through the use of varied instructional and curricular adaptations. Saint Xavier University. (ERIC Reproduction Service ED 412006)

Flynn, J. R. (1987). Massive IQ gains in 14 nations: what IQ tests really measure. *Psychological Bulletin, 101*, 171-191.

Flynn, J. R. (1994). IQ gains over time. In R. J. Sternberg (Ed.), *Encyclopedia of human intelligence* (pp. 617-623). New York: Macmillan.

Gardner, H. (1983). *Frames of mind: The theory of multiple intelligences*. New York: Basics.

Gottfried, A. E., & Gottfried, A. W. (1996). A longitudinal study of academic intrinsic motivation in intellectually gifted children: Childhood through early adolescence. *Gifted Child Quarterly, 40*, 179-183.

Gregorc, A. (1982). *An adult's guide to style*. Columbia, CT: Gregorc Associates.

Guild, P. B., & Garger, S. (1985). *Marching to different drummers*. Alexandria, VA: Association for Supervision and Curriculum Development.

Guilford, J. P. (1959). Three faces of intellect. *American Psychologist, 14*, 469-479.

Harter, S. (1992). The relationship between perceived competence, affect, and motivational orientation within the classroom: Processes and patterns of change. In A. K. Boggiano & T. S. Pittman (Eds.), *Achievement and motivation: A social-developmental perspective* (pp. 77-114). New York: Cambridge University Press.

Herrnstein, R. J., & Murray, C. (1994). *The bell curve*. New York: Free Press.

Hunt, D. E. (1971). *Matching models in education: The coordination of teaching methods with student characteristics*. Ontario, Canada: Ontario Institute for Studies in Education.

James, N. E. (1962). Personal preference for method as a factor in learning. *Journal of Educational Psychology, 53*, 43-47.

Joyce, B. R., & Hodges, R. E. (1966). Instruction flexibility training. *Journal of Teacher Education, 17*, 409-416.

Joyce, B. R., & Weil, M. (1972). *Models of teaching*. Englewood Cliffs, NJ: Prentice-Hall.

Kuhl, J. (1985). Volitional mediators of cognition-behavior consistency: Self-regulatory processes and action versus state orientation. In J. Kuhl & J. Beckmann (Eds.), *Action control: From cognition to behavior* (pp. 101-128). Berlin: Springer.

Lesser, G. S. (1971). Matching instruction to student characteristics. In Lesser, G. S. (Ed.), *Psychology and educational practice*. Glenview, IL: Scott, Foresman.

Lewis, M. D. (1989). Early infant-mother interaction as a predictor of problem-solving in toddlers. *International Journal of Early Childhood, 21*, 13-22.

Loewenstein, G. (1994). The psychology of curiosity: A review and reinterpretation. *Psychological Bulletin, 116*, 75-98.

Lohman, D. F. (1993). Teaching and testing to develop fluid abilities. *Educational Researcher, 22*(7), 12-23.

Mac Iver, D. J., Stipek, D. J., & Daniels, D. H. (1991). Explaining within-semester changes in student effort in junior high school and senior high school courses. *Journal of Educational Psychology, 83*, 201-211.

McCarthy, B. (1980). *The 4MAT system: Teaching to learning styles with right/left mode techniques*. Barrington, IL: Excel.

McCarthy, B. (1990, October). Using the 4MAT system to bring learning styles to schools. *Educational Leadership*, 31-37.

McNamee, G. E. (1971). Instructional stereotypes and educational practice. In Lesser, G. S. (Ed.), *Psychology and educational practice*. Glenview, IL: Scott, Foresman.

Myers, I. B., & Briggs, K. C. (1976). *The Meyers-Briggs type indicator*. Palo Alto, CA: Consulting Psychologists Press, Inc.

Newell, A., & Simon, H. A. (1972). *Human problem solving*. Englewood Cliffs, NJ: Prentice Hall.

Pascal, C. E. (1971). Instructional options, option preferences and course outcomes. *The Alberta Journal of Educational Research, 17,* 1-11.

Phenix, P. H. (1987). *Views on the use, misuse, and abuse of instructional materials*. Paper presented at the Annual Meeting of the Leadership Training Institute on the Gifted and Talented, Houston, TX.

Piaget, J. (1967). *Six psychological studies*. New York: Random House.

Plomin, R., & Petrill, S. A. (1997). Genetics and intelligence: What's new? *Intelligence, 24,* 53-77.

Prenzel, M. (1992). The selective persistence of interest. In K. A. Renninger, S. Hidi, & A. Krapp (Eds.), *The role of interest in learning and development* (pp. 71-98). Hillsdale, NJ: Lawrence Erlbaum Associates.

Purcell, J. H., & Renzulli, J. S. (1998). *Total talent portfolio: A systematic plan to identify and nurture gifts and talents*. Mansfield Center, CT: Creative Learning Press.

Reis, S. M., Burns, D. E., & Renzulli, J. S. (1992). *Curriculum compacting: The complete guide to modifying the regular curriculum for high-ability students*. Mansfield Center, CT: Creative Learning Press.

Renzulli, J. S. (1977). *The Interest-A-Lyzer*. Mansfield Center, CT: Creative Learning Press.

Renzulli, J. S. (1992). A general theory for the development of creative productivity in young people. In F. Monks, W. Peters (Eds.), *Talent for the future: Social and personality development of gifted children* (pp. 51-72). Assen/Maastricht, The Netherlands: Van Gorcum.

Renzulli, J. S. (1994). *Schools for talent development: A practical plan for total school improvement*. Mansfield Center, CT: Creative Learning Press.

Renzulli, J. S. (1997). *The Interest-A-Lyzer family of instruments: A manual for teachers*. Mansfield Center, CT: Creative Learning Press.

Renzulli, J. S., & Dai, D. Y. (2001). Abilities, interests, and styles as aptitudes for learning: A person-situation interaction perspective. In Sternberg, R. J., & Zhang, L. (Eds.). *Perspectives on thinking, learning, and cognitive styles* (pp. 23-46). London: Lawrence Earlbaum.

Renzulli, J. S., & Reis, S. M. (1985). *The schoolwide enrichment model: A comprehensive plan for educational excellence*. Mansfield Center, CT: Creative Learning Press.

Renzulli, J. S., & Reis, S. M. (1997). *The schoolwide enrichment model: A how-to guide for educational excellence (2nd ed.)*. Manchester Center, CT: Creative Learning Press.

Renzulli, J. S., & Smith, L. H. (1984). Learning style preferences: A practical approach for classroom teachers. *Theory Into Practice, 18*, 44-50.

Renzulli, J. S., & Smith, L. H. (1978). *Learning Styles Inventory: A measure of student preference for instruction techniques.* Mansfield Center, CT: Creative Learning Press.

Rosenberg, M. B. (1968). *Diagnostic teaching.* Seattle, WA: Special Child Publications.

Schunk, D. H., & Zimmerman, B. J. (Eds.). (1994). *Self-regulation of learning and performance: Issues and educational applications.* Hillsdale, NJ: Lawrence Erlbaum Associates, Inc.

Smith, L. H. (1976). *Learning styles: Measurement and educational significance.* Unpublished doctoral dissertation, University of Connecticut, Storrs.

Snow, R. E. (1992). Aptitude theory: Yesterday, today, and tomorrow. *Educational Psychologist, 27*, 5-32.

Stahl, S. A., & Kuhn, M. R. (1995). Does whole language or instruction matched to learning styles help children learn to read? *School Psychology Review, 24*, 393-404.

Starko, A. J. (1986). *The effects of the revolving door identification model on creativity and self efficacy.* Unpublished doctoral dissertation, University of Connecticut, Storrs.

Stednitz, U. (1985). *The influence of educational enrichment on the self-efficacy in young children.* Unpublished doctoral dissertation, University of Connecticut, Storrs.

Sternberg, R. J. (1985). *Human intelligence: An information-processing approach.* New York: Freeman.

Sternberg, R. J. (1988). Mental self-government: A theory of intellectual styles and their development. *Human Development, 31*, 197-221.

Sternberg, R. J. (1998). Abilities are forms of developing expertise. *Educational Researcher, 27*(3), 11-20.

Sternberg, R. J., & Kaufman, J. C. (1998). Human abilities. *Annual Review of Psychology, 49*, 479-502.

Tannenbaum, A. (1962). *Adolescents' attitudes toward academic brilliance.* New York: Bureau of Publications, Teachers College, Columbia University.

Tanner, L. N. & Lindgren, H. C. (1971). *Classroom teaching and learning: A mental health approach.* New York: Holt, Rinehart & Winston.

Thomas, A., & Chess, S. (1977). *Temperament and development.* New York: Bruner/Mazel.

Torrance, E. P. (1965). Different ways of learning for different kinds of children. In E. P. Torrance & R. D. Strom (Eds.), *Mental health and achievement: Increasing potential and reducing school dropout.* New York: Wiley.

Vinton, J. (1968). *The relationship among life style, task and structure in university classrooms.* Unpublished doctoral dissertation, Case Western Reserve University, Cleveland, OH.

White, R. W. (1959). Motivation reconsidered: The concept of competence. *Psychological Review, 66*, 297-333.

Zimmerman, B. J. (1990). A social cognitive view of self-regulated academic learning. *Journal of Educational Psychology, 81*, 329-339.

APPENDIX B

In Appendix B, we present a method for gathering and maintaining information about students abilities, interests, and styles in a Total Talent Portfolio. Teachers can use this information to make informed decisions about providing enrichment experiences to students.

LOOKING AT THE WHOLE STUDENT: DEVELOPING A TOTAL TALENT PORTFOLIO

Every learner has strengths or potential strengths that can serve as a foundation for effective learning and creative productivity, and any model for total talent development (e.g., Schoolwide Enrichment Model (Renzulli & Reis, 1997) requires that educators give equal attention to interests and learning styles as well as to the cognitive abilities traditionally used for educational decision making. The Total Talent Portfolio (Purcell & Renzulli, 1998) provides educators with a format for systematically gathering and recording information about students' abilities, interests, and learning styles. With this information, teachers gain a more complete picture of a student upon which they can structure more appropriate learning experiences. The major purposes of the Total Talent Portfolio are:

1. To **collect** several different types of information that portray a student's strength areas and to update this information regularly.

2. To **classify** this information into the general categories such as abilities, interests, and style preferences.

3. To **review and analyze** the information periodically in order to make purposeful decisions about providing opportunities for enrichment experiences in the regular curriculum, enrichment clusters, and continuum of special services.

4. To **negotiate** various acceleration and enrichment learning options and opportunities between teacher and student through participation in a shared decision-making process.

5. To **use the information** as a vehicle for educational, personal, and career counseling and for communicating with parents about the school's talent development opportunities and their child's involvement in them.

The dimensions of the portfolio that guide data gathering and the specific items included in each dimension are presented in Figure 1. Because one goal of the TTP is to encourage students to take ownership of their work and their education, students should assume primary responsibility for selecting items to include, maintaining and regularly updating the portfolio, and setting personal goals. Teachers, then, serve as guides in the portfolio review process and use this information to make decisions about future enrichment and talent development experiences for the student.

The unique feature of the Total Talent Portfolio is its focus on strengths and "high-end learning" behaviors. A tradition exists in education that has caused us to use student records mainly for spotting deficiencies. Our adherence to the medical (i.e., diagnostic-prescriptive) model has almost always been pointed in the negative direction: "Find out what's wrong with them and fix them up!" Total talent assessment emphasizes the identification of the most positive aspects of each student's learning behaviors. The portfolio should include all information that calls attention to strong interests, preferred styles of learning, and high levels of motivation, creativity and leadership as well as the academic strengths that can be used as stepping stones to more advanced learning activities.

Abilities	Interests	Style Preferences			
Maximum Performance Indicators	Interest Areas[2]	Instructional Style Preferences[3]	Learning Environment Preferences[5]	Thinking Style Preferences[6]	Expression Style Preferences[7]
Tests	Fine Arts	Recitation & Drill	**Inter-/Intrapersonal**	Analytic (school smart)	Written
• Standardized	Crafts	Peer Tutoring	• Self-oriented	Synthetic/Creative (creative, inventive)	Oral
• Teacher-Made	Literary	Lecture	• Peer-oriented	Practical/Contextual (street smart)	Manipulative
Course Grades	Historical	Lecture/Discussion	• Adult-oriented		Discussion
Teacher Ratings	Mathematical/Logical	Discussion	• Combined	Legislative	Display
Product Evaluation[1]	Physical Sciences	Guided Independent Study[4]	**Physical**	Executive	Dramatization
• Written	Life Sciences	Learning/Interest Center	• Sounds	Judicial	Artistic
• Oral	Political/Judicial	Simulation, Role Playing, Dramatization, Guided Fantasy	• Heat		Graphic
• Visual	Athletic/Recreation	Learning Games	• Light		Commercial
• Muscial	Marketing/Business	Replicative Reports or Projects[4]	• Design		Service
• Constructed	Drama/Dance	Investigative Reports or Projects[4]	• Mobility		
Level of participation in learning activities	Muscial Performance	Unguided Independent Study[4]	• Time of Day		
Degree of interaction with others	Musical Composition	Internship	• Food Intake		
	Managerial/Business	Apprenticeship	• Seating		
	Photography				
	Film/Video				
	Computers				
	Others (Specify)				

[1] Note difference between assigned and self-selected products.
[2] Ref. Renzulli, 1997
[3] Ref. Renzulli, Smith, & Rizza, 2002
[4] With or without a mentor

[5] Ref. Amabile, 1983; Dunn, Dunn, & Price, 1977; Gardner, 1983
[6] Ref. Sternberg, 1984, 1988, 1990
[7] Ref. Kettle, Renzulli, & Rizza, 1998; Renzulli & Reia, 1985

Figure 1. Dimensions of the Total Talent Portfolio

Status Information

The first type of information recorded in the TTP deals with student assets in the areas of abilities, interests, and learning styles commonly called status information. Status information is anything educators know or can record about a student prior to the instructional process that tells them something about learner characteristics. Examples of status information are test scores, course grades, teacher ratings of various learning behaviors, and formal and informal assessments of interests and learning styles.

<u>Abilities</u>

Abilities, or maximum performance indicators (as traditionally defined in the psychometric literature), deal with competencies that represent the highest level of performance a student has attained in a particular area of aptitude or scholastic achievement. Assessment on this dimension of school performance has traditionally been evaluated by tests or course grades. The first column of Figure 1 includes these conventional assessments, but it also includes a number of additional procedures by which educators can examine maximum performance. These procedures may not be as reliable and objective as traditional tests, but they do have the advantage of letting teachers know how students perform on more complex tasks and on tasks that require the application of knowledge to assigned or self-selected learning activities.

While the merits of formal testing versus alternative forms of assessment have been debated extensively in the literature, we believe that any and all sources of information are valuable if they improve teacher understanding of potential for future performance and if they provide direction for enhancing future performance. We believe that alternative forms of assessment are equal in value to formal tests, and a Total Talent Portfolio that does not include alternate assessment information will be limited. Teacher-made assessments provide information about knowledge acquisition, the mastery of basic skills, and, in some cases, problem-solving strategies. This information is valuable for determining general levels of proficiency, but the most valuable kind of teacher-made assessments, so far as the purposes of the Total Talent Portfolio are concerned, are those that elicit open-ended or extended responses. Responses of this type enable teachers to gain insight into complex student abilities such as constructing convincing arguments, using expressive written or oral language, generating relevant hypotheses, applying creative solutions to complex problems, and demonstrating deep levels of understanding. Open-ended responses also provide excellent opportunities for students to demonstrate artistic and scientific creativity and to display advanced abilities such as analysis, generalization, and evaluation.

The grades students have received in previously completed courses and work products can also provide information about particular strength areas. When grades reflect both performance on teacher-made assessments and other accomplishments in less structured situations, they provide a more comprehensive picture of student abilities than can be derived from test scores alone. The advantages and disadvantages of course grades are well documented in the literature on tests and measurements, and all teachers have had experiences related to the grading process and the usefulness of grades. The value of course grades in the Total Talent Portfolio is similar to standardized and teacher-made assessments in that they all provide a quick overview of general area strengths that may be capitalized upon when making decisions about possible modifications in the regular curriculum, enrichment cluster placement, or access to special opportunities that are available in the continuum of special services.

A teacher-rating instrument such as the *Scales for Rating the Behavioral Characteristics of Superior Students—Revised Edition* (2002) can also provide insight into student abilities and talents. Although the *Scales* are traditionally used to identify students for special services, schools and teachers should not shy away from using them in a TTP as a way to gain more complete pictures of student strengths.   Because these scales assess strengths in nonacademic areas such as leadership, music, drama, motivation, and creativity, they add to the total student picture in a way more traditional assessments would not.   Sample pages from the *Scales* appear in Appendix C.

Interests

Building educational experiences around student interests is probably one of the most effective ways to guarantee that enrichment practices will be introduced into a school. In numerous evaluation studies of Schoolwide Enrichment Model programs, student comments about most favored practices almost always dealt with greater freedom for selecting at least a part of the work they pursued based on their interests. A planned strategy for helping students examine their present and potential interests is based on a group of instruments called the *Interest-A-Lyzer* (Renzulli, 1977, 1997). The *Interest-A-Lyzer* family of instruments is available in three levels, Primary (K-3), Elementary (3-6), and Secondary (7-12), as well as in the area of art, and sample pages from each are included in Appendix C.

The main purpose of the *Interest-A-Lyzer* is to open up communication both within the student and between students and teachers. It also is designed to facilitate discussion between groups of students with similar interests who are attempting to identify areas in which they might like to pursue advanced level studies. The *Interest-A-Lyzer* is not the type of instrument that yields a numerical score; it is designed to allow for *pattern analysis*. The major patterns or factors that might emerge from the instrument include:

1. Performing Arts
2. Creative Writing and Journalism
3. Mathematics
4. Business Management
5. Athletics
6. History
7. Social Action
8. Fine Arts and Crafts
9. Science
10. Technology

It is important to keep in mind that the above factors represent *general* fields or families of interest and that numerous ways exist in which an individual may be interested in any particular field. Thus, identifying general patterns is only the first step in interest analysis. General interests must be refined and focused so that students identify specific problems within a general field or combination of fields that interest them.

Instructional Styles Preferences

The third column of Figure 1 lists a broad range of instructional techniques that are familiar to most teachers. The version of the *Learning Styles Inventory* presented in this manual can help teachers identify the learning styles their students prefer. While including learning style preferences in the TTP is important, teachers should be careful not to label a child with a learning style. While a very few students will prefer one instruction style over all others for all curriculum areas and through their educational career, most students will vary their preferences according to subject and age. Educators should reassess student preferences periodically and include the updated information in the TTP.

Learning Environmental Preferences

Environmental preferences have not been investigated to the same extent as preferences for instructional style; however, a small body of research and a large measure of common sense suggest that the social and physical aspects of the environment affect various kinds of school performance. Amabile (1983) reviewed research dealing with social and environmental factors that influence creativity in school-age learners. Some students thrive in small or large peer group situations, others prefer to work with a single partner, and still others prefer to work alone or with an adult. Environmental preferences, like instructional preferences, may vary as a function of the material being taught, the nature of the task to be accomplished, and the social relationships that exist within any given group of students. Although a predominant organizational arrangement may be necessary for purposes of efficiency and classroom control, teachers should consider some variety when it is clear that some students will benefit from an alternative learning environment.

Thinking Styles Preferences

The fifth dimension of the Total Talent Portfolio provides information about the ways in which learners prefer to use their abilities and aptitudes. Thinking styles preferences might best be viewed as the bridge between abilities and personality, and information about this dimension of the learner provides direction about the ways in which students like to address problems. Sternberg (1988) uses the three branches of the U.S. Government as a metaphor for the theory of mental self-government. The *legislative* function of mind is concerned with creating, formulating, and planning. Persons with a legislative style like to create their own rules and ways of doing things, and they prefer less structured problems and constructive, planning-based activities such as writing original works, building things, and designing new projects or enterprises. People with this style enter occupations such as creative writing, science, art, investment banking, policy making, and architecture. The *executive* function is concerned with carrying out or implementing plans or ideas initiated by others. Persons with an executive style prefer to follow rules, figure out ways to get things done, and they like prestructured problems and working within existing structures. The executive style may be the preferred learning style among lawyers, builders, surgeons, policemen, managers, and administrators. The *judicial* function involves monitoring problems and passing judgment over ideas or products. Persons with a judicial style like to evaluate rules, procedures, and existing structures, they like to write critiques, give opinions, and judge people and their work. This style is found in occupations such as judge, critic, systems analyst, admissions officer, and quality control specialist (Sternberg, 1988).

Sternberg and Wagner (1991) developed and carried out research studies on an instrument entitled, *Mental Self-Government Thinking Styles Inventory*. This 128-item, Likert scale questionnaire yields factor scores for each of the following 13 subscales: Legislative, Executive, Judicial, Global, Local, Progressive, Conservative, Hierarchical, Monarchical, Oligarchic, Anarchic, Internal, and External.

Expression Style Preferences

The final category in the Total Talent Portfolio deals with the ways in which people prefer to express themselves. Most classroom activities depend on written, computational, and oral expression. Special subject areas such as art and physical education are based on expression styles inherent in their respective disciplines. However, knowledge of expression style preferences can help teachers expand the range of learning options for individuals and small groups by "legitimizing" a broader variety of expressions from leadership-oriented expressions to product-oriented expressions. If students have a choice in the manner in which they present their understanding and competence in an area, their interest in a particular expression style may serve to motivate them to higher levels of productivity and learning. Furthermore, knowledge of the ways in which young people prefer to express themselves can be a valuable tool for organizing cooperative learning and project groups. By varying responsibilities along the lines of expression styles, a functional rather than random division of labor is established, and more students have an opportunity to contribute in unique strength areas.

An instrument entitled *My Way: An Expression Styles Inventory* (Kettle, Renzulli, & Rizza, 1998) has been developed to help teachers and students identify preferences for products. Research is being conducted on the secondary version of the instrument which is designed to yield the following 10 categories: Written, Oral, Artistic, Computer Technology, Audio/Visual Technology, Commercial, Service, Dramatization, Manipulative, and Musical. A sample of this instrument is included in Appendix C.

Action Information

Action information consists of annotated recordings of events that take place within the instructional process. By definition, action information cannot be recorded beforehand because it is designed to document the ways in which students react to various learning experiences as well as other experiences that take place outside the formal learning environment.

By observing and documenting performance, satisfaction, and enthusiasm, educators can make decisions about subsequent activities that will capitalize on positive reactions to previous experiences. The TTP serves as a format for documenting these reactions so that staff members along with parents and students can make decisions about appropriate follow-up, needed resources, and the development of future performance assessment situations.

Action information also consists of annotated work samples of completed assignments and other performance-based observations and assessments. These annotations can be informal notes as well as more structured analyses of student work. Because students select items for the portfolio, teachers must reinforce important process skills in analysis and evaluation. Some teachers have developed rating sheets that students complete and hand in with the project. These rubrics allow students the opportunity to learn how to learn, to understand exactly what standards are being set for them, and to evaluate their work objectively.

Using the Total Talent Portfolio

The main purpose of the Total Talent Portfolio is to provide a comprehensive picture of each student's strengths in the areas of abilities, interests, and styles. Student work, selected by teachers *and* students, should be placed in the portfolio, and both teachers and students should make note of examples of particular strengths within a work sample with attached notes or comments written in the margins of the work. Teams of teachers should review portfolios periodically, and the portfolios should serve as focal points for meetings with parents. The portfolio should travel with students from year to year and should serve as the basis for briefing subsequent year teachers about individual student strengths and accomplishments.

Unlike the cumulative folder, the TTP contains specific information about student strengths that often lies hidden within test scores and course grades. It contains tangible pieces of information about a student that completes a 3-dimensional picture of that student. It forces the reader to focus on the positive, individual strengths of that student in order to gain a better understanding of how to help her or him learn. Above all, the Total Talent Portfolio is a place where teachers, students, and parents can share ideas to make the most of the educational experience.

Teachers and other school personnel teach because they want to make positive a difference in the lives of young people. Parents, too, want to see their children provided with challenging learning opportunities that build upon and develop their strengths. Yet many teachers and parents struggle separately to ensure students' access to high-end learning opportunities. The Total Talent Portfolio provides a unique framework that invites parents, students, and teachers to work together to identify students' strengths and talents. From the information gathered in the TTP, teachers can help students make the most of their "best things"—abilities, interests, and style preferences—by providing students with challenging experiences that engage young people's minds and inspire them to learn and create.

REFERENCES

Amabile, T. M. (1983). *The social psychology of creativity.* New York: Springer-Verlag.

Purcell, J. H., & Renzulli, J. S. (1998). *Total talent portfolio: A systematic plan to identify and nurture gifts and talents.* Mansfield Center, CT: Creative Learning Press.

Kettle, K. E., Renzulli, J. S., & Rizza, M. G. (1998). Products of mind: Exploring student preferences for product development using *My Way: An Expression Style Inventory. Gifted Child Quarterly, 42* (1), 48-61.

Renzulli, J. S. (1977). *The Interest-A-Lyzer.* Mansfield Center, CT: Creative Learning Press.

Renzulli, J. S. (1997). *The Interest-A-Lyzer family of instruments: A manual for teachers.* Mansfield Center, CT: Creative Learning Press.

Renzulli, J. S., & Reis, S. M. (1997). *The Schoolwide Enrichment Model: A comprehensive plan for educational excellence.* Mansfield Center, CT: Creative Learning Press.

Renzulli, J. S., Smith, L. H., White, A. J., Callahan, C. M., Hartman, R. K., & Westberg, K. L. (2002). *Scales for Rating the Behavioral Characteristics of Superior Students—Revised Edition.* Mansfield Center, CT: Creative Learning Press.

Sternberg, R. J. (1988). Mental self-government: A theory of intellectual styles and their development. *Human Development, 31,* 197-224.

Sternberg, R. J., & Wagner, R. K. (1991). *Mental self-government thinking styles inventory.* New Haven, CT: Authors.

APPENDIX C

In this appendix, we include sample pages from a variety of instruments that, along with the *LSI-III*, can help teachers develop more complete pictures of their students. Appendix B outlines how teachers can put this information together in a Total Talent Portfolio.

Scales for Rating Behavioral Characteristics of Superior Students (Grades 3-12)

SCALES FOR RATING THE BEHAVIORAL CHARACTERISTICS OF SUPERIOR STUDENTS

Joseph S. Renzulli / Linda H. Smith / Alan J. White / Carolyn M. Callahan / Robert K. Hartman / Karen L. Westberg

---

Directions: These scales are designed to obtain teacher estimates of a student's characteristics in the areas of Learning, Motivation, Creativity, Leadership, Art, Music, Drama, Communication, and Planning. The items are derived from the research literature dealing with characteristics of gifted and creative individuals. It should be pointed out that a considerable amount of individual differences can be found within this population, and therefore, the profiles are likely to vary a great deal. Each item in the scales should be considered separately and should reflect the degree to which you have observed the presence or absence of each characteristic. Since the ten dimensions of the instrument represent relatively different sets of behaviors, the scores obtained from the separate scales should *not* be summed to yield a total score. In addition, we have purposefully avoided developing national norms for this instrument. If you choose to develop local norms, they should be constructed for individual schools and grade levels.

Read each item in each scale and place an "**X**" in the box that corresponds with the frequency to which you have observed the behavior. Each item should be read with the beginning phrase, "**The student demonstrates . . .**" or "**The student . . .**"

Scoring:
- Add the total number of **X**'s in each column to obtain the "Column Total."
- Multiply the "Column Total" by the "Weight" for each column to obtain the "Weighted Column Total."
- Sum the "Weighted Column Totals" across to obtain the Score for each dimension of the scale.
- Enter the Scores below.

I	**Learning Characteristics**	_____
II	**Creativity Characteristics**	_____
III	**Motivation Characteristics**	_____
IV	**Leadership Characteristics**	_____
V	**Artistic Characteristics**	_____
VI	**Musical Characteristics**	_____
VII	**Dramatics Characteristics**	_____
VIII	**Communication Characteristics (Precision)**	_____
IX	**Communication Characteristics (Expressiveness)**	_____
X	**Planning Characteristics**	_____

Scales for Rating Behavioral Characteristics of Superior Students (Grades 3-12)

CREATIVITY CHARACTERISTICS

The student demonstrates . . .	Never	Very Rarely	Rarely	Occasionally	Frequently	Always
1. imaginative thinking ability.	☐	☐	☐	☐	☐	☐
2. a sense of humor.	☐	☐	☐	☐	☐	☐
3. the ability to come up with unusual, unique, or clever responses.	☐	☐	☐	☐	☐	☐
4. an adventurous spirit or a willingness to take risks.	☐	☐	☐	☐	☐	☐
5. the ability to generate a large number of ideas or solutions to problems or questions.	☐	☐	☐	☐	☐	☐
6. a tendency to see humor in situations that may not appear to be humorous to others.	☐	☐	☐	☐	☐	☐
7. the ability to adapt, improve or modify objects or ideas.	☐	☐	☐	☐	☐	☐
8. intellectual playfulness, willingness to fantasize and manipulate ideas.	☐	☐	☐	☐	☐	☐
9. a non-conforming attitude, does not fear being different.	☐	☐	☐	☐	☐	☐
Add Column Total	☐	☐	☐	☐	☐	☐
Multiply by Weight	1	2	3	4	5	6
Add Weighted Column Totals	☐ +	☐ +	☐ +	☐ +	☐ +	☐
Scale Total						☐

Scales for Rating Behavioral Characteristics of Superior Students (Grades 3-12)

MOTIVATION CHARACTERISTICS

The student demonstrates . . .	Never	Very Rarely	Rarely	Occasionally	Frequently	Always
1. the ability to concentrate intently on a topic for a long period of time.	☐	☐	☐	☐	☐	☐
2. behavior that requires little direction from teachers.	☐	☐	☐	☐	☐	☐
3. sustained interest in certain topics or problems.	☐	☐	☐	☐	☐	☐
4. tenacity for finding out information on topics of interest.	☐	☐	☐	☐	☐	☐
5. persistent work on tasks even when setbacks occur.	☐	☐	☐	☐	☐	☐
6. a preference for situations in which he or she can take personal responsibility for the outcomes of his or her efforts.	☐	☐	☐	☐	☐	☐
7. follow-through behavior when interested in a topic or problem.	☐	☐	☐	☐	☐	☐
8. intense involvement in certain topics or problems.	☐	☐	☐	☐	☐	☐
9. a commitment to long term projects when interested in a topic.	☐	☐	☐	☐	☐	☐
10. persistence when pursuing goals.	☐	☐	☐	☐	☐	☐
11. little need for external motivation to follow through in work that is initially exciting.	☐	☐	☐	☐	☐	☐
Add Column Total	☐	☐	☐	☐	☐	☐
Multiply by Weight	1	2	3	4	5	6
Add Weighted Column Totals	☐ +	☐ +	☐ +	☐ +	☐ +	☐
Scale Total						☐

Primary Interest-A-Lyzer (Grades K-3)

PRIMARY INTEREST-A-LYZER

By
Joseph S. Renzulli
and Mary G. Rizza
University of Connecticut

Name:_____ **Age:**_____

Teacher:_____ **Date:**_____

Note to Teachers & Parents:

This *Interest-A-Lyzer* is designed for students in grades K-3. It is intended for whole classroom use but some students, especially those who cannot read, may need some individual attention for proper completion. Picture cues are provided for each question to help keep new readers on task and to facilitate with group administration. It is suggested that an adult consult with students and annotate the responses, particularly when students use inventive spelling. This will facilitate interpretation and ensure proper identification later on.

Interpretation of this instrument is similar to other versions of the *Interest-A-Lyzer* and will look at individual responses within the context of broader categories. The more information obtained from the child, the easier it will be to interpret. Whenever necessary, the student should be asked to provide more information by asking questions like "Why?" or "How long?" or "Is that all?" It is hoped that teachers will view this instrument as an opportunity to interact with their students on a positive and enjoyable activity. We feel it is a great way to get to know your students and their non-academic interests.

Remember that there are no right or wrong answers to this instrument and special attention should be given to ensure that each response is true to the student's own unique interests. There are no time limits for completion. In fact, students should be encouraged to think about their answers before filling out this instrument.

Primary Interest-A-Lyzer (Grades K-3)

What kinds of books do you like to read?

_____

_____

_____

_____

What is your favorite book?

_____

_____

Do you belong to any clubs or teams?

Tell about them here:

_____

_____

_____

_____

Imagine that you can travel to any time in history.

Where would you go?

_____

_____

_____

_____

_____

Primary Interest-A-Lyzer (Grades K-3)

Lots of people play games. What are some of your favorite games?

_____

_____

Have you ever made up a new game? Tell about it here:

_____

_____

_____

Pretend your class is going on a trip and you are in charge of picking the place to go.

Check off 3 ideas from below.

_____ Museum   _____ Science Center

_____ Sports Game   _____ A Show like Ice Capades

_____ Music Concert   _____ Mayor's Office

_____ Newspaper Office   _____ Firehouse

_____ T.V. Studio   _____ Planetarium

_____ Court Room   _____ Police Station

_____ The Zoo   _____ An Amusement Park

_____ A Play

What did we forget? _____

Interest-A-Lyzer (Grades 4-8)

The Interest-A-Lyzer

by
Joseph S. Renzulli
University of Connecticut

Name _____   Age _____

School _____   Grade _____

                                             Date _____

The purpose of this questionnaire is to help you become more familiar with some of your interests and potential interests. The questionnaire is not a test and there are no right or wrong answers. Your answers will be completely confidential. You may want to talk them over with your teacher or other students, but this choice is entirely up to you.

Some of the time that you spend on enrichment activities will be devoted to working on individual or small group projects. We would like you to work on projects that are of interest to you, so it is necessary for you to do a little thinking to know what some of your interests might be.

A good way for you to get in touch with your interests is to think about some of the things you like to do now and also some of the things you might like to do if the given the opportunity. Some of the questions that follow will be "Imagine if..." questions, but keep in mind that their only purpose is to have you think about the choices you would make in an imaginary situation.

As you read the questions try not to think about the kinds of answers that your friends might write or how they might feel about your answers. Remember, no one will see your answers if you want to keep them confidential.

Do not try to answer the questions now. Read them over and think about them for a few days and then write your answers. Please do not discuss the questionnaire with others at this time. Sometimes we can be influenced by the opinions of others and this influence may prevent you from exploring some of your own interests. Remember, the purpose of The Interest -A-Lyzer is to get YOU to THINK about YOUR OWN INTERESTS.

Interest-A-Lyzer (Grades 4-8)

1. Imagine that your class has decided to create its own Video Production Company. Each person has been asked to sign up for his or her first, second or third choice for one of the jobs listed below. Mark your first choice with a 1, second choice with a 2, and third choice with a 3.

_____ Actor/Actress

_____ Director

_____ Musician

_____ Business Manager   _____ Costume Designer

_____ Computer Effects Specialist   _____ Scenery Designer

_____ Prop Person   _____ Light/Sound Person

_____ Advertising Agent   _____ Camera Operator

_____ Script Writer   _____ Dancer

SAMPLE

2. Imagine that you have become a famous author of a well-known book. What is the general subject of your book? Circle One.

Fine Arts   Business   Science

Writing   History   Social Action

Athletics   Mathematics

Performing Arts   Technology

What will it be about?

_____

_____

_____

_____

What would be a good title for your book?

_____

Interest-A-Lyzer (Grades 4-8)

3. Computers and telephone technology allow us to communicate with people all over the world. Imagine that your school has installed an Internet or telephone system that will allow you to communicate with anyone in the world. With whom would you correspond?

First Choice _____

Second Choice _____

Third Choice _____

4. Imagine that a time machine has been invented that will allow famous people from the past to travel through time. If you could invite some of these people to visit your class, who would you invite?

First Choice _____

Second Choice _____

Third Choice _____

5. Are you a collector? Do you collect stamps, coins, autographs, baseball cards, or other things? List the things that you collect and the number of years you have been collecting.

Things I Collect	Number of Years I Have Been Collecting
_____	_____
_____	_____
_____	_____
_____	_____

Imagine you have the time and the money to collect anything you wanted. What would you collect?

_____

_____

Secondary Interest-A-Lyzer **(Grades 7-12)**

Secondary

Interest-A-Lyzer

Thomas P. Hébert
The University of Alabama

Michele F. Sorensen
Berlin, Connecticut Public Schools

Joseph S. Renzulli
The University of Connecticut

This is an informal interest inventory that will serve as a foundation for developing your specific areas of interest throughout the school year. The information you provide is completely confidential. As a result of this survey, we hope to provide you with meaningful educational experiences that will further develop your interests, nurture your talents, and challenge your learning potential.

Read each question carefully and provide us with as much detailed information as possible so we may obtain a clear understanding of your interests.

Name _____

Grade _____   Date _____

School _____

Secondary Interest-A-Lyzer (Grades 7-12)

1 You are fed up with the course offerings at your high school. Your principal has asked you to design the perfect course for people with your same interests. What would the course be called? What would be taught?

2 Rather than provide money for a class trip, the board of education has decided to give money to each individual student for a trip of his or her choice! Where would you go? List three (3) places you would visit and explain what you would do while visiting there. Why?

3 You have written your first book which you are ready to submit for publication. What is the title? What is the book about?

4 You have been asked to plan a concert for your high school. You have an unlimited budget! List three (3) choices of musical performances that you would schedule for that evening's program.

My Way: An Expression Style Inventory (Grades 6-9)

My Way ...

An Expression Style Inventory
K. E. Kettle, J. S. Renzulli, M. G. Rizza
University of Connecticut

Products provide students and professionals with a way to express what they have learned to an audience. This survey will help determine the kinds of products **YOU** are **interested** in creating.

My Name is: _____

Instructions:

Read each statement and circle the number that shows to what extent **YOU** are **interested** in creating that type of product. (Do not worry if you are unsure of how to make the product.)

		Not At All Interested	A Little Interested	Moderately Interested	Interested	Very Interested
	Example: writing song lyrics		2	3	(4)	5
1.	writing stories	1	2	3	4	5
2.	discussing what I have learned	1	2	3	4	5
3.	painting a picture	1	2	3	4	5
4.	designing a computer software project	1	2	3	4	5
5.	filming & editing a video	1	2	3	4	5
6.	creating a company	1	2	3	4	5
7.	helping in the community	1	2	3	4	5
8.	acting in a play	1	2	3	4	5

My Way: An Expression Style Inventory (Grades 6-9)

		Not At All Interested	Of Little Interest	Moderately Interested	Interested	Very Interested
43.	making a clay sculpture of a scene	1	2	3	4	5
44.	designing a multi-media computer show	1	2	3	4	5
45.	selecting slides & music for a slide show	1	2	3	4	5
46.	managing investments	1	2	3	4	5
47.	collecting clothing or food to help others	1	2	3	4	5
48.	role-playing a character	1	2	3	4	5
49.	assembling a kit	1	2	3	4	5
50.	playing in an orchestra	1	2	3	4	5

The End

My Way... A Profile

Instructions: Write your score beside each number. Add each <u>ROW</u> to determine <u>YOUR</u> expression style profile.

<u>Products</u>

						Total
Written	1. ___	11. ___	21. ___	31. ___	41. ___	___
Oral	2. ___	12. ___	22. ___	32. ___	42. ___	___
Artistic	3. ___	13. ___	23. ___	33. ___	43. ___	___
Computer	4. ___	14. ___	24. ___	34. ___	44. ___	___
Audio/Visual	5. ___	15. ___	25. ___	35. ___	45. ___	___
Commercial	6. ___	16. ___	26. ___	36. ___	46. ___	___
Service	7. ___	17. ___	27. ___	37. ___	47. ___	___
Dramatization	8. ___	18. ___	28. ___	38. ___	48. ___	___
Manipulative	9. ___	19. ___	29. ___	39. ___	49. ___	___
Musical	10. ___	20. ___	30. ___	40. ___	50. ___	___

APPENDIX D

Appendix D presents non-reproducible samples of all three instruments included in the *Learning Styles Inventory, Version III*. To obtain classroom sets of the Elementary School instrument or the Middle School instrument, please contact Creative Learning Press, Inc. Each classroom set includes 30 student instruments, 1 teacher instrument, and 1 classroom summary sheet.

Elementary School Instrument

The Learning Styles Inventory **Version III – ES**
J.S. Renzulli, L.H. Smith, & M.G. Rizza

My Name: _____ **My Grade:** _____

Directions: Read each sentence and decide if it describes an activity that you would like to do in school. For each sentence circle the number that goes with how well you like or dislike each activity. Remember this is not about what you get to do in school, but what you would like to do. Be sure to mark an answer for each of the sentences. After each section, add up your score. When you are finished, locate your score in the chart on the last page as directed by your teacher.

I.

	Really Like	Like	Not Sure	Dislike	Really Dislike
1-1. Listen to your teacher explain new information.	4	3	2	1	0
1-2. Have the teacher give specific instructions on how to do things.	4	3	2	1	0
1-3. Have the teacher make clear what is expected of the class.	4	3	2	1	0
1-4. Listen as your teacher presents a lesson.	4	3	2	1	0
1-5. Have the teacher lead a discussion on a new topic.	4	3	2	1	0
1-6. Hear the teacher present information to the class.	4	3	2	1	0
1-7. Listen to your teacher present various points of view on a subject.	4	3	2	1	0
1-8. Have the teacher review what students should know.	4	3	2	1	0

Section I Total Score _____

II.

	Really Like	Like	Not Sure	Dislike	Really Dislike
2-1. Use a computer program to solve a problem.	4	3	2	1	0
2-2. Use a computer program to learn new information.	4	3	2	1	0
2-3. Watch a video with a narrator who explains new information.	4	3	2	1	0
2-4. Participate in a chat room or newsgroup over the Internet in which you discuss topics of interest.	4	3	2	1	0
2-5. Watch a broadcast of a program to learn more on a topic you are studying in class.	4	3	2	1	0
2-6. Work on activities that use the computer to help you learn information.	4	3	2	1	0
2-7. Use a computer program that helps you review information you need to know for class.	4	3	2	1	0
2-8. Use the Internet to find information to help you with a project you are working on for class.	4	3	2	1	0
2-9. Participate in an interactive activity over the Internet.	4	3	2	1	0

Section II Total Score _____

Elementary School Instrument

The Learning Styles Inventory **Version III – ES**
J.S. Renzulli, L.H. Smith, & M.G. Rizza

III.	Really Like	Like	Not Sure	Dislike	Really Dislike
3-1. Learn about an event such as the signing of the Declaration of Independence by acting it out in class.	4	3	2	1	0
3-2. Learn about the election process by playing the role of a member of a campaign team.	4	3	2	1	0
3-3. Learn about possible careers by acting out the role of a job counselor and interviewing other students who are acting as job applicants.	4	3	2	1	0
3-4. Learn how government works by playing the role of an official working with a local citizen group.	4	3	2	1	0
3-5. Work with a committee to prepare a lesson to present to the class.	4	3	2	1	0
3-6. Interview adults about careers you are interested in pursuing.	4		2	1	0
3-7. Role play the part of a famous person whose life interests you.	4		2	1	0
3-8. Act out the part of scientist, journalist, artist or some other professional person.	4	3	2	1	0

Section III Total Score _____

IV.	Really Like	Like	Not Sure	Dislike	Really Dislike
4-1. Study on your own to learn new information.	4	3	2	1	0
4-2. Plan a project to work on by yourself.	4	3	2	1	0
4-3. Work on your own to prepare material you will present to the class.	4	3	2	1	0
4-4. Read a book to learn all about a topic you select.	4	3	2	1	0
4-5. Work on your own to study a topic you choose.	4	3	2	1	0
4-6. Work independently on a project you choose yourself.	4	3	2	1	0
4-7. Work by yourself to collect information on a topic of interest.	4	3	2	1	0
4-8. Go to the library by yourself to find more information about a topic.	4	3	2	1	0

Section IV Total Score _____

Elementary School Instrument

V.	Really Like	Like	Not Sure	Dislike	Really Dislike
5-1. Work with other students on a project with little help from your teacher.	4	3	2	1	0
5-2. Discuss class material with a group of other students.	4	3	2	1	0
5-3. Work with other students on a project the teacher suggests.	4	3	2	1	0
5-4. Work with other students to plan a project about a topic in class.	4	3	2	1	0
5-5. Work with other students in planning and completing a project.	4	3	2	1	0
5-6. Prepare a written report with a committee.	4	3	2	1	0
5-7. Work with other students on a special project based on something that interests you.	4	3	2	1	0
5-8. Go to the library with a committee to find information.	4	3	2	1	0
5-9. Talk with other students in your class about a topic of interest.	4	3	2	1	0

Section V Total Score _____

VI.	Really Like	Like	Not Sure	Dislike	Really Dislike
6-1. Have a friend help you learn difficult material.	4	3	2	1	0
6-2. Have a classmate teach you how to do something he or she does well.	4	3	2	1	0
6-3. Learn new information from another student in your class.	4	3	2	1	0
6-4. Have a student in your grade work with you to review material for a test.	4	3	2	1	0
6-5. Work in the back of your classroom with another student who will help you with schoolwork.	4	3	2	1	0

Section VI Total Score _____

Elementary School Instrument

The Learning Styles Inventory

Version III – ES

J.S. Renzulli, L.H. Smith, & M.G. Rizza

VII.

	Really Like	Like	Not Sure	Dislike	Really Dislike
7-1. Be quizzed by your teacher to see if you understand a story you read.	4	3	2	1	0
7-2. Fill in the missing word to complete a sentence on an assignment.	4	3	2	1	0
7-3. Have a spelling bee with other students in your class.	4	3	2	1	0
7-4. Do assignments in which you find out after each question whether your answer is correct.	4	3	2	1	0
7-5. Have a contest to see if your team can correctly answer questions about a topic you are studying in class.	4	3	2	1	0
7-6. Work on assignments that have questions that you can correct on your own.	4	3	2	1	0
7-7. Have your teacher call on individual students to recite information that you have learned.	4	3	2	1	0
7-8. Have the teacher call on individual students by name to answer questions.	4	3	2	1	0
7-9. Have the teacher ask questions to see what you have learned.	4	3	2	1	0

Section VII Total Score _____

			Section Totals				Converted Score
I.	II.	III.	IV.	V.	VI.	VII.	
31 - 32	36	31 - 32	30 - 32	34 - 36	19 - 20	33 - 36	10
28 - 30	33 - 35	28 - 30	27 - 29	31 - 33	17 - 18	30 - 32	9
25 - 27	30 - 32	25 - 27	24 - 26	28 - 30	15 - 16	27 - 29	8
22 - 24	27 - 29	22 - 24	21 - 23	25 - 27	13 - 14	23 - 26	7
19 - 21	24 - 26	19 - 21	17 - 20	22 - 24	11 - 12	20 - 22	6
16 - 18	21 - 23	16 - 18	14 - 16	19 - 21	9 - 10	17 - 19	5
12 - 15	18 - 20	12 - 15	11 - 13	16 - 18	7 - 8	14 - 16	4
9 - 11	15 - 17	9 - 11	8 - 10	13 -15	5 - 6	11 - 13	3
5 - 8	12 - 14	5 - 8	5 - 7	10 - 12	3 - 4	8 - 10	2
0 - 4	0 - 11	0 - 4	0 - 4	0 -9	0 - 2	0 - 7	1
Direct Instruction	Instruction through Technology	Simulations	Independent Study	Projects	Peer Teaching	Drill & Recitation	

Middle School Instrument

The Learning Styles Inventory — Version III – MS
J.S. Renzulli, L.H. Smith, & M.G. Rizza

My Name: _____   My Grade: _____

<u>Directions:</u> Read each sentence and decide if it describes an activity that you would like to do in school. For each sentence circle the number that goes with how well you like or dislike each activity. Remember this is not about what you get to do in school, but what you would like to do. Be sure to mark an answer for each of the sentences. After each section, add up your score. When you are finished, locate your score in the chart on the last page as directed by your teacher.

I.

	Really Like	Like	Not Sure	Dislike	Really Dislike
1-1. Listen to your teacher explain new information.	4	3	2	1	0
1-2. Have the teacher give specific instructions on how to do things.	4	3	2	1	0
1-3. Have the teacher make clear what is expected of the class.	4	3	2	1	0
1-4. Listen as your teacher presents a lesson.	4	3	2	1	0
1-5. Have the teacher lead a discussion on a new topic.	4	3	2	1	0
1-6. Hear the teacher present information to the class.	4	3	2	1	0
1-7. Listen to your teacher present various points of view on a subject.	4	3	2	1	0
1-8. Have the teacher review what students should know.	4	3	2	1	0
1-9. Take notes as the teacher talks to the class.	4	3	2	1	0
1-10. Have the teacher ask questions to see what you have learned.	4	3	2	1	0

Section I Total Score _____

II.

	Really Like	Like	Not Sure	Dislike	Really Dislike
2-1. Use a computer program to solve a problem.	4	3	2	1	0
2-2. Use a computer program to learn new information.	4	3	2	1	0
2-3. Watch a video with a narrator who explains new information.	4	3	2	1	0
2-4. Participate in a chat room or newsgroup over the Internet in which you discuss topics of interest.	4	3	2	1	0
2-5. Watch a broadcast of a program to learn more on a topic you are studying in class.	4	3	2	1	0
2-6. Work on activities that use the computer to help you learn information.	4	3	2	1	0
2-7. Use a computer program that helps you review information you need to know for class.	4	3	2	1	0
2-8. Use the Internet to find information to help you with a project you are working on for class.	4	3	2	1	0
2-9. Participate in an interactive activity over the Internet.	4	3	2	1	0
2-10. Exchange e-mail with someone about a topic of mutual interest.	4	3	2	1	0

Section II Total Score _____

Middle School Instrument

The Learning Styles Inventory   **Version III – MS**

J.S. Renzulli, L.H. Smith, & M.G. Rizza

III.	Really Like	Like	Not Sure	Dislike	Really Dislike
3-1. Learn about an event such as the signing of the Declaration of Independence by acting it out in class.	4	3	2	1	0
3-2. Learn about the election process by playing the role of a member of a campaign team.	4	3	2	1	0
3-3. Learn about possible careers by acting out the role of a job counselor and interviewing other students who are acting as job applicants.	4	3	2	1	0
3-4. Learn how government works by playing the role of an official working with a local citizen group.	4	3	2	1	0
3-5. Work with a committee to prepare a lesson to present to the class.	4	3	2	1	0
3-6. Interview adults about careers you are interested in pursuing.	4	3	2	1	0
3-7. Role play the part of a famous person whose life interests you.	4	3	2	1	0
3-8. Act out the part of scientist, journalist, artist or some other professional person.	4	3	2	1	0

Section III Total Score _____

IV.	Really Like	Like	Not Sure	Dislike	Really Dislike
4-1. Study on your own to learn new information.	4	3	2	1	0
4-2. Plan a project to work on by yourself.	4	3	2	1	0
4-3. Work on your own to prepare material you will present to the class.	4	3	2	1	0
4-4. Read a book to learn all about a topic you select.	4	3	2	1	0
4-5. Work on your own to study a topic you choose.	4	3	2	1	0
4-6. Work independently on a project you choose yourself.	4	3	2	1	0
4-7. Work by yourself to collect information on a topic of interest.	4	3	2	1	0
4-8. Go to the library by yourself to find more information about a topic.	4	3	2	1	0

Section IV Total Score _____

SAMPLE

Middle School Instrument

The Learning Styles Inventory
Version III – MS
J.S. Renzulli, L.H. Smith, & M.G. Rizza

V.	Really Like	Like	Not Sure	Dislike	Really Dislike
5-1. Work with other students on a project with little help from your teacher.	4	3	2	1	0
5-2. Discuss class material with a group of other students.	4	3	2	1	0
5-3. Work with other students on a project the teacher suggests.	4	3	2	1	0
5-4. Work with other students to plan a project about a topic in class.	4	3	2	1	0
5-5. Work with other students in planning and completing a project.	4	3	2	1	0
5-6. Prepare a written report with a committee.	4	3	2	1	0
5-7. Work with other students on a special project based on something that interests you.	4	3	2	1	0
5-8. Participate in a group in which everyone has a different role and helps each other with their work.	4	3	2	1	0

Section V Total Score _____

VI.	Really Like	Like	Not Sure	Dislike	Really Dislike
6-1. Have a friend help you learn difficult material.	4	3	2	1	0
6-2. Have a classmate teach you how to do something he or she does well.	4	3	2	1	0
6-3. Learn new information from another student in your class.	4	3	2	1	0
6-4. Have a student in your grade work with you to review material for a test.	4	3	2	1	0
6-5. Work in the back of your classroom with another student who will help you with schoolwork.	4	3	2	1	0
6-6. Work with a classmate to review homework assignments.	4	3	2	1	0

Section VI Total Score _____

VII.	Really Like	Like	Not Sure	Dislike	Really Dislike
7-1. Have a class discussion on a topic suggested by the teacher.	4	3	2	1	0
7-2. Have other students present their ideas to the class.	4	3	2	1	0
7-3. Hear the ideas of other students during a class discussion of an assigned topic.	4	3	2	1	0
7-4. Share ideas with other students during a class discussion.	4	3	2	1	0
7-5. Listen to classmates give their opinions on a subject.	4	3	2	1	0
7-6. Talk with other students in your class about a topic of interest.	4	3	2	1	0

Section VII Total Score _____

Middle School Instrument

The Learning Styles Inventory
Version III – MS
J.S. Renzulli, L.H. Smith, & M.G. Rizza

VIII.	Really Like	Like	Not Sure	Dislike	Really Dislike
8-1. Play a board game to help practice one of your school subjects.	4	3	2	1	0
8-2. Practice vocabulary words by playing a word game.	4	3	2	1	0
8-3. Play a game using flash cards in order to practice what you have learned.	4	3	2	1	0
8-4. Have a spelling bee with other students in your class.	4	3	2	1	0
8-5. Have a contest to see if your team can correctly answer questions about a topic you are studying in class.	4	3	2	1	0
8-6. Participate in a game that tests your knowledge of material you have learned.	4	3	2	1	0

Section VIII Total Score _____

SAMPLE

			Section Totals					Converted Score
I.	II.	III.	IV.	V.	VI.	VII.	VIII.	
36 - 40	39 - 40	31 - 32	28 - 32	29 - 32	22 - 24	21 - 24	23 - 24	10
32 - 35	37 - 38	28 - 30	25 - 27	26 - 28	20 - 21	19 - 20	21 - 22	9
28 - 31	33- 36	25 - 27	21 - 24	23 - 25	18 - 19	17 - 18	19 - 20	8
24 - 27	29 - 32	22 - 24	18 - 20	20 - 22	16 - 17	15 - 16	17 - 18	7
19 - 23	25 - 28	19 - 21	14 - 17	17 - 19	14 - 15	13 - 14	15 - 16	6
15 - 18	21 - 24	16 - 18	11 - 13	14 - 16	12 - 13	11 - 12	13 - 14	5
11 - 14	17 - 20	12 - 15	8 - 10	11 - 13	10 - 11	9 - 10	11 - 12	4
7 - 10	13 - 16	9 - 11	4 - 7	8 - 10	8 - 9	7 - 8	9 - 10	3
3 - 6	9 - 12	5 - 8	1 - 3	5 - 7	6 - 7	5 - 6	7 - 8	2
0 - 2	0 - 8	0 - 4	0 - 2	0 - 4	0 - 5	0 - 4	0 - 6	1
Direct Instruction	Instruction through Technology	Simulations	Independent Study	Projects	Peer Teaching	Discussion	Teaching Games	

Teacher Instrument

- -
The Learning Styles Inventory   **Version III – Teacher**
- -
                                                       J.S. Renzulli, L.H. Smith, & M.G. Rizza

This instrument mirrors the *Learning Styles Inventory* instruments for students. An "(es)" or "(ms)" following an item indicates that the particular item is found only on elementary school instrument (es) or middle school instrument (ms). Elementary school teachers should respond to "(es)" items, and middle school teachers should respond to "(ms)" items. All teachers should respond to the remaining items as they are found on both instruments. Please read each item and decide how often these events occur in your classroom. After each section, add up your score and divide by the number of items in the factor. For information on interpreting your score, see Part I of the *Learning Styles Inventory, Version III Technical and Administration Manual*.

I.

	Daily	Weekly	Monthly	Occasionally	Never
1-1. Explain new information while the students listen.	4	3	2	1	0
1-2. Give specific instructions on how to do things.	4	3	2	1	0
1-3. Make clear what is expected of the class.	4	3	2	1	0
1-4. Have students listen as you present a lesson.	4	3	2	1	0
1-5. Lead a discussion with students on a new topic.	4	3	2	1	0
1-6. Have students listen as you present information to the class.	4	3	2	1	0
1-7. Have students listen to you present various points of view on a subject.	4	3	2	1	0
1-8. Review what students should know.	4	3	2	1	0
1-9. Ask questions of the students to see what they have learned. (es)	4	3	2	1	0
1-10. Have students take notes as you talk to the class. (ms)	4	3	2	1	0

Direct Instruction Score _____ ÷ 8 (es) or 10 (ms) = _____

II.

	Daily	Weekly	Monthly	Occasionally	Never
2-1. Have students use a computer program to solve a problem.	4	3	2	1	0
2-2. Have students use a computer program to learn new information.	4	3	2	1	0
2-3. Have students watch a video with a narrator who explains new information.	4	3	2	1	0
2-4. Have students participate in a chat room or newsgroup over the Internet in which they discuss about topics of their interest.	4	3	2	1	0
2-5. Have students watch a broadcast of a program to learn more about a topic being studied in class.	4	3	2	1	0
2-6. Have students work on activities that use the computer to help them learn information.	4	3	2	1	0
2-7. Have students use a computer program that helps them review information needed for class.	4	3	2	1	0
2-8. Have students use the Internet to find information to help with a project they are working on for class.	4	3	2	1	0
2-9. Have students participate in an interactive activity over the Internet.	4	3	2	1	0
2-10. Have students exchange e-mail with someone about a topic of mutual interest. (ms)	4	3	2	1	0

Information through Technology Score _____ ÷ 9 (es) or 10 (ms) = _____

Teacher Instrument

The Learning Styles Inventory   **Version III – Teacher**

J.S. Renzulli, L.H. Smith, & M.G. Rizza

III.

	Daily	Weekly	Monthly	Occasionally	Never
3-1. Teach about an event such as the signing of the Declaration of Independence by having students acting it out in class.	4	3	2	1	0
3-2. Teach about the election process by having students play the roles of a campaign team.	4	3	2	1	0
3-3. Teach about possible careers by having students act out the role of a job counselor and interview other students who are acting as job applicants.	4	3	2	1	0
3-4. Teach how government works by having students play the role of an official working with a local citizen group.	4	3	2	1	0
3-5. Have students work in a committee to prepare a lesson to present to the class.	4	3	2	1	0
3-6. Have students interview adults about careers they are interested in pursuing.	4	3	2	1	0
3-7. Have students role play the part of a famous person whose life interests them.	4	3	2	1	0
3-8. Have the students act out the part of scientist, journalist, artist or some other professional person.		3	2	1	0

Simulations Score _____ ÷ 8 = _____

IV.

	Daily	Weekly	Monthly	Occasionally	Never
4-1. Have students study on their own to learn new information.	4	3	2	1	0
4-2. Have students plan a project to work on by themselves.	4	3	2	1	0
4-3. Have students work on their own to prepare material they will present to the class.	4	3	2	1	0
4-4. Have students read a book to learn about a topic the student selects.	4	3	2	1	0
4-5. Have students work on their own to study a topic they choose.	4	3	2	1	0
4-6. Have students work independently on a project they choose.	4	3	2	1	0
4-7. Have students work alone to collect information on a topic of interest.	4	3	2	1	0
4-8. Have students go to the library alone to find more information about a topic.	4	3	2	1	0

Independent Study Score _____ ÷ 8 = _____

Teacher Instrument

••
• The Learning Styles Inventory   Version III – Teacher •
• J.S. Renzulli, L.H. Smith, & M.G. Rizza **•**
••

V.	Daily	Weekly	Monthly	Occasionally	Never
5-1. Have students work on a project with little help from you.	4	3	2	1	0
5-2. Have students discuss class material in a small group.	4	3	2	1	0
5-3. Have students work together on a project that you suggest.	4	3	2	1	0
5-4. Have students work in a group to plan a project on a topic in class.	4	3	2	1	0
5-5. Have students work together to plan and complete a project.	4	3	2	1	0
5-6. Have students prepare a written report with a committee.	4	3	2	1	0
5-7. Have students work together on a special project based on something that interests them.	4	3	2	1	0
5-8. Have students go to the library with a committee to find information. (es)	4	3	2	1	0
5-9. Have students talk with others in the class about a topic of interest. (es)	4	3	2	1	0
5-10. Have students participate in a group in which everyone has a different role and helps each other with their work. (ms)	4	3	2	1	0

Projects Score _____ ÷ 9 (es) or 8 (ms) = _____

VI.	Daily	Weekly	Monthly	Occasionally	Never
6-1. Have friends work together to learn difficult material.	4	3	2	1	0
6-2. Have classmates teach each other how to do something he or she does well.	4	3	2	1	0
6-3. Have students learn new information from other students in the class.	4	3	2	1	0
6-4. Have students in your grade work together to review material for a test.	4	3	2	1	0
6-5. Let students work in the back of your classroom who will help each other with schoolwork.	4	3	2	1	0
6-6. Have classmates work together to review homework assignments. (ms)	4	3	2	1	0

Peer Teaching Score _____ ÷ 5 (es) or 6 (ms) = _____

Teacher Instrument

The Learning Styles Inventory   **Version III – Teacher**
J.S. Renzulli, L.H. Smith, & M.G. Rizza

VII-ES.

	Daily	Weekly	Monthly	Occasionally	Never
7-1. Quiz students to see if they understand a story that they read.	4	3	2	1	0
7-2. Have students fill in the missing word to complete a sentence on an assignment.	4	3	2	1	0
7-3. Have a spelling bee with the class.	4	3	2	1	0
7-4. Have students do assignments in which they find out after each question whether their answer is correct.	4	3	2	1	0
7-5. Have a contest to see if one team can correctly answer questions about a topic being studied in class.	4	3	2	1	0
7-6. Have students work on assignments with questions that they can correct on their own.	4	3	2	1	0
7-7. Call on students to recite information that they have learned.	4	3	2	1	0
7-8. Call on students by name to answer questions.	4	3	2	1	0
7-9. Ask students questions to see what they have learned.	4		2	1	0

Drill & Recitation Score _____ ÷ 9 = _____

VII-MS.

	Daily	Weekly	Monthly	Occasionally	Never
7-1. Have a class discussion on a topic you suggest.	4	3	2	1	0
7-2. Have students present their ideas to the class.	4	3	2	1	0
7-3. Have students listen to the ideas of others during a class discussion of an assigned topic.	4	3	2	1	0
7-4. Have students share ideas with each other during a class discussion.	4	3	2	1	0
7-5. Have students listen to classmates give their opinions on a subject.	4	3	2	1	0
7-6. Have students talk with each other about a topic of interest.	4	3	2	1	0

Discussion Score _____ ÷ 6 = _____

VIII-MS.

	Daily	Weekly	Monthly	Occasionally	Never
8-1. Have students play board games that help them practice school subjects.	4	3	2	1	0
8-2. Have students play a word game to practice vocabulary words.	4	3	2	1	0
8-3. Have students play a game using flash cards to practice what they have learned.	4	3	2	1	0
8-4. Have a spelling bee with the class.	4	3	2	1	0
8-5. Have a contest to see if one team can correctly answer questions about a topic being studied in class.	4	3	2	1	0
8-6. Play a game that tests students' knowledge of material they have learned.	4	3	2	1	0

Teaching Games Score _____ ÷ 6 = _____